Gottlieb Christopher Henry Hasskarl

How did the Universe Originate and When did the World Become a Habitable Earth?

The True Answer in the Light of the Hebrew and Greek Scriptures

Gottlieb Christopher Henry Hasskarl

How did the Universe Originate and When did the World Become a Habitable Earth?
The True Answer in the Light of the Hebrew and Greek Scriptures

ISBN/EAN: 9783337420277

Printed in Europe, USA, Canada, Australia, Japan

Cover: Foto ©ninafisch / pixelio.de

More available books at **www.hansebooks.com**

How Did The Universe Originate

AND

When Did The World Become A Habitable Earth?

THE TRUE ANSWER

IN

THE LIGHT OF THE HEBREW AND GREEK SCRIPTURES.

READ BEFORE

THE NATIONAL ACADEMY OF THEOLOGY.

———

Sketches on a Few of The Great Problems of Science,
Philosophy, and Theology,

BY

REV. G. C. H. HASSKARL, PH. D.,

Member of the American Association for the Advancement of Science, and
Member of the National Academy of Theology, and Author of "The
Word of God, Systematical and Daily;" "The Terrible Catastrophe
or Biblical Deluge;" "Evolution, As Taught In the Bible;"
"The Church's Triumph In The Formation and Adoption
of The Augsburg Confession;" "The Sanctuary, Its
Origin, Design, and Importance."

———

FOR SALE AT THE LUTHERAN PUBLICATION HOUSE, 42 NORTH
9TH STREET, PHILADELPHIA, PA.

CONTENTS.

CHAPTER I.

The Difficulties,............................... Page 5

CHAPTER II.

The Creation of The Elements,................. Page 11

CHAPTER III.

The Origin of the Universe,................... Page 30

CHAPTER IV.

The Appearance of Light...................... Page 42

CHAPTER V.

The Earth's Canopy and Strata................ Page 50

CHAPTER VI.

Seas. Continents and Vegetation.............. Page 59

CHAPTER VII.

The Light-Bearers,........................... Page 69

CHAPTER VIII.

Sea-Monsters and Birds,...................... Page 77

CHAPTER IX.

Beast, Cattle and Man,....................... Page 85

Index,....................... .... Page 99

CHAPTER I.

Perhaps no subjects have engaged the attention of the peasant and the King, the mind of the philosopher and the theologian, ancient, mediaeval and modern, more intensely, than the subjects of the first twelve chapters of the Book Genesis. The first and second chapters give the genesis of the Universe; the third and fourth chapters reveal the genesis of Sin; the sixth and following chapters describe the destruction of a wicked race and the preservation of one family; the tenth and eleventh chapters contain the genesis of the Nations, and have remained to this day an authority on that subject among Ethnologists; the twelfth chapter presents the genesis of the Abrahamic people. It is, indeed, a book of generations, births, beginnings and origins.

And these stupendous facts and sublime truths,—particularly those concerning the origin of the Universe and of man—how have they been treated by writer after writer, and expounded by one commentator after another? Have the facts not been explained away by amazing perversions, and the truths contained therein ignored by mere theories. And why all this? Simply because men quite too frequently are disposed to put modern notions and unwarranted constructions on very ancient language, and that, of the most sacred and valuable fragment of antiquity. The only Cosmogony (1) that survives all others which are the mere fabric of men's fancy, unreal and untrue.

Again, "cultivators of science—professors and amateurs —are doing not a little to loosen its authority, and especially to imperil if not destroy its educational value, by neglecting to draw the boundary line sharply round its true domain. A great deal conventionally passes under the name, which is no more science than bricks and timber are a building. It is *art*—the art of making science. The facts patiently accumulated, accurately analyzed and recorded, on which, step by step, scientific inductions are raised are the precious material of science: but they are not science. The keen eye of the naturalist; the adroit and sensitive finger of the operator; the insight, imagination, and ready invention which mark the man of scientific genius from the mere plodder, and enable him to look behind the veil before he persuades Nature herself to lift it; these are admirable, invaluable, indispensable to the progress of science. But they are not science. Theories and hypothesis—the shelves on which we pack and label our facts, the luggage vans in which we forward them on their journey—are among the most useful implements of scientific discovery. But they are not science. Above all, the dicta of individual scientists, how eminent soever, are not science. To claim for

---

1. If we have a true cosmogony and a partially false religion, why just as sure as a truth of the cosmogony comes in contact with a false part of religion there will be a clash. But one cosmogony and one religion are one and the same thing. Otherwise our entire cosmogony might exactly as well have been formulated by an atheist.—*The Author.*

what at best can but rank as 'pious opinions' the authority of infallible dogma, is both disloyal to truth and perilous to intellectual freedom.

"For, be it remembered, liberty of thought—a phrase which often stands for much liberty but little thought—is inconsistent with science. Where science begins liberty ends. Any one is at liberty either to think that two ultimate atoms of matter can occupy the same space, or to think that they are impenetrable, mutually excluding one another. This liberty results from our present ignorance. But no one is at liberty to think that the angles of a plane triangle can be less than two right angles, or that they can be greater; because we certainly know them to be equal. Liberty of thought, is not even the path, of which science is the goal. It is simply the throwing down of all hedges and walls, and banishment of all threatening notices, watch-dogs, patrols, and man-traps, whereby our right to explore the waste was limited; so that we are free to make our own path as the stars guide us. But we take our own risk of bogs and precipices. Doubt may unlock the fetters of tradition, and start us, with its sharp spur deep in our heart, in quest of truth. But it guides us no step of the way; and in presence of ascertained truth it expires. The freedom of inquiry, and of provisional belief or disbelief, which is the condition of honestly working out a scientific deduction or induction, become irrational when once the result is known. Much nonsense about intellectual liberty might have been spared, if people would bear in mind the obvious fact that free thought and science are mutually inconsistent. The one supposes the absence of the other. Hence the immense

importance of not *anticipating science* by erecting into
dogma the theories, conjectures, or personal opinions of
scientific leaders." (1)

This "anticipating science by erecting into dogma the
theories, conjectures, or personal opinions of scientific leaders" has not been indulged time and again by professed
scientists alone; but even by such as profess to believe in
the Scriptures,—accepting and adopting them in all their
teachings. When we come to examine the foundation of
their belief, expecting to find it honest and sincere, we are
pained to discover a wretched self-deception,—fancy of a
belief the mere ground supposed to be on the Scripture, but
after all resting altogether for its main support on some loud
scientist or philosopher. These are no doubt unintentional
errors which men make by not accepting the Scriptures in
the sense and for the purpose for which they were divinely
given. But how are men misled, and what is the cause of
it? Simply this: when the book of a human author is
read, they do not charge themselves with the task of cor-
recting its language with the idea of bringing it into a
more complete harmony with the author's thought. The
author is held responsible for his work, and the conceptions
contained therein, and would doubtless feel highly dishon-
ored were his *pupils* to add to or take aught from his passages, with the avowed intent of making clearer his meaning. And yet, this is just what men have been disposed
to do with the first twelve chapters of the book Genesis,

---

1. *The Scientific Evidences of Organic Evolution, by George J. Romanes,
A. M., LL. D., F. R. S.,* p. 40, *H. L. Ed.*

particularly with the account of the origin of the Universe and of man. Instead of believing and holding God responsible for the language in which He has been pleased to express Himself, make manifest His works, and reveal His designs; —which constitute a revelation of His power, good will and divine Mind, they have created for themselves endless trouble by reading into the Scriptures what is nowhere to be found,—terrestrially or celestially.

That the minds of many good men should thus at times become uneasy under the suspicion of a conflict between the Book of Nature and the Book of God need hardly surprise us. Yet, a moment's reflection on their part would have removed all the difficulties, for they know that the commandments given to Moses on Mount Sinai more than endorse the original account of the Creation, and of which Christ Himself makes mention, and which is accepted also by *all* the inspired writers. The sooner therefore men will abandon everything that is contrary to the Scriptures, the sooner and better will they understand and adopt their teachings which refer to the material Universe, and all that concerns man, his origin, his purpose, and his destiny. For truth is the agreement of thought and speech with the reality of facts and things. (1) And nowhere is this more obvious than in the first two chapters of Genesis, which we have endeavored to interpret and present in the light of the Hebrew and Greek Scriptures; for the purpose of showing . how even here Scripture serves itself as the best commentary on Scripture. It is the only truly self-interpreting

---

1. Truth is to thought, what logic, which is the ordered sequence of conscious experience, is to reason.—*The Author*.

Book among books, and the sooner men are convinced of the truth of this fact, the higher will it stand even in the estimation of the world-wise;—they will discover therein "what are the first principles of every science." (1) Besides, the believing will the more value it and consider it the more sacred, knowing that its contents are in truth a revelation from God unto man.   And neither aged, nor young men of good education, after thoroughly understanding the Scripture conception and interpretation of the centre and of the circumference of Creation, need any longer be disquieted in their minds, if not really unsettled in their religious principles, by the results of scientific investigation, no more than by any other seeming difficulty attending revealed truth. It is for the latter class in particular that we have attempted to give *the creative feature alone;* and thus shall endeavor to set forth some of the first principles involved in the Sacred narrative of Creation, so full of mystery, and so full of wonder.

---

1. Professor Henry Drummond defends the Bible record in Genesis in the following unique way: "Men could find out the order in which the world was made. What they could not find out, was that God made it. To this day they have not found that out. Even some of the wisest of our contemporaries, after trying to find that out for half a lifetime, have been forced to give it up. Hence the true function of Revelation. Nature in Genesis has no link with geology, seeks none and needs none : man has no link with biology, and misses none. What he really needs and really misses—for he can get it nowhere else—Genesis gives him ; it links nature and man with their Maker. And this is the one high sense in which Genesis can be said to be scientific. The scientific man must go there to complete his science, or it remains forever incomplete. Let him no longer resort thither to attack what is not really there. What is really there he cannot attack, for he cannot do without it."—*Evolution as Taught in the Bible, etc., by Rev. G. C. H. Hasskarl, p.* 35.

CHAPTER II.

GEN. I : I.

"*In the beginning*," on the first instant of time "*God created*" (Heb. BARA—to create) instantaneously by the purpose and goodness of His Will (1) from nothing *outside* of Himself the very substance (Heb. AYTH) in essentia of the "*the heavens*" (Heb. HASHAMAYIM) "*and*" (Heb. VE AYTH) the substance in essentia of "*the earth*" (Heb. HAARETS).   (2)

It is not a little remarkable that the Spirit of God should direct Moses to open the Sacred Volume with a literal description of the origin of the physical Universe, its systems, and suns, and stars. A record "vast in its outlines, it is

---

1. " In the primeval creation there was no instrumental cause or means, because God created all things by the Word."—*Calovius.*

"Neither was there any antecedent cause, except the purpose of God alone, communicating Himself, not from the necessity of nature, but from the freedom of His Will."—*Quenstcd.*

" The impelling cause of creation is the immense goodness, from which God, as He wished to communicate the highest good, most freely communicated Himself."—*Calovius.*

2. " This simple sentence denies *atheism*; for it assumes the being of God. It denies *polytheism*, and, among its various forms, the doctrine of two eternal principles, the one good and the other evil; for it confesses the

yet so scrupulously strict in its minuter details, that it may
be read without dubiety, not only in the midst of the exact-
est records of antiquity, but in the light of those modern
discoveries in physical science which bear most directly on
its statements.''

We do not purpose here to prove the existence of a God
and Creator, for this the Bible assumes and every intelligent

---

"Creation is a free, divine action, because God framed the universe,
not induced thereto by necessity, as though He needed the service of creatures, since He is absolutely independent (*autarkestatos*), but freely, as He
was able to create, and not to create and to frame, sooner or later, in this
or in another manner."—*Hollazius.*

"Hence creation is also described as not successive, but, with respect
to every individual being created, instantaneous, for God framed everything, not by any movement or laborious exertion, but when He said, 'Let
there be light,' immediately there was light."—*Hollazius.*

"The action is not properly successive, but instantaneous; for the indi-
viduals, which God created, He created in an instant, without movement
or succession, although, if these be regarded collectively, the creation was
completed in six days (*nuchdemera*); not that He devoted those entire days
to creation, but that He created something in the moments of each day."—
*Calovious, in The Doctrinal Theology of the Evangelical Lutheran Church, by
Dr's Hay and Jacobs, p. 170, 2nd Edition.*

The difficulty on our part of comprehending the Divine creating and
moving, commanding and naming, seeing and approving, working and
resting here in creation, must not discredit the truth which agrees with
facts. For, while it is a well grounded basis of belief and action, that man
is endowed with a spirit, yet, he cannot comprehend that spirit any more
than reason or thought, mind or life. Again, if the most highly endowed
among men were asked the question of their natural origin and development, not to mention the psychological, they could never give the true
answer, were they ignorant of the necessary natural conditions of the
origin and development, no more than they could judge the contents of an
egg by its shell.—*The Author.*

one Eternal Creator. It denies *materialism*, for it asserts the creation of
matter. It denies *pantheism*, for it assumes the existence of God before all
things, and apart from them. It denies *fatalism*, for it involves the freedom of the eternal being."—*The Terrible Catastrophe or Biblical Deluge, etc.,
by Rev. G. C. H. Hasskarl, Ph. D., p. 240.*

person believes, knowing that nothing comes from nobody, nor from nothing when the the crude material is manifest everywhere in nature. But rather to inquire into the processes and the order of development by which the Universe was made to assume the material forms which it reveals. In order to erect a structure of any kind, there must be materials, there must be the power to move and fix these materials. The architect, of course, must know of what material he means to build, and its stability; what kind of power he intends using, and its amount. And that the Architect of the Universe did not create "the worlds" from anything *outside* of Himself scarcely needs here to be mentioned. For those who advocate the eternity of space and time, matter and motion, all of them dependent one upon another; might as well affirm that chemistry or electricity or gravity or any other power or law known to man are all isolated and alone, self-made and self-born substances or manifestations. Nor need we be told that when God intended, by the purpose and goodness of His unconditioned, conditionating Will and Power building, that he did not at once in "the beginning" on the first instant of time, originate the very substance *in essentia*—primordial elements out of which "the heavens and the earth"—Universe and world were afterwards to be "framed by the word of God;" (1) or be informed that

---

1. "*Was ist für Gott das Weltall? Sein Werk, seine Schoepfung* nennt es die Schrift; denn Gottes ist die Kraft, wodurch alles entsteht and besteht, in ihm, nicht in sich selber, aus ihm, aus der goettichen Lebens fulle hat das Weltall sein Leben, and Gott ist eben darin Schoepfer, kein Werkmeister, dasz er ihm rein aus dem eigenen Schatze wie gemaesz dem eigenen Willen alle Kraft, alles Leben verliehen hat (Rom. 11:36; Rev, 4:11; Job 33:4; Neh. 9:6; Acts 17, 24 ff). Die Welterschaffung ist nach der Schriftlehre

the Universe was not created all at once; but that there was a certain order (1) in which the various parts appeared, is clearly affirmed in the creative record, and is evident also from the discoveries of science;—is expressed, in fact, in the very language which the inspired penman uses.

---

kein unmittelbares Werk des goettlichen Willens, wird vielmehr *durch goettliches Wrot vermittelt*. Nun brauchen wir kaum die Bemerkung beizufugen, dasz unverkennbar hierunter kein hoerbarer Laut zu verstechen (comp. Hebr. 1:3; with 11:2); dennoch *scheint* es, Gott werde hiermit in der Aenlichkeit des Menschen gedacht, dessen Gedanke nicht den Vollzug einschlieszt, sondern eines bestimmteu Ausdruckes bedarf, um in der Auszenwelt sich zur Geltung zu bringen. Allein wie, wenn zwar Gott zum Werke des Sprechens nicht bedurfte, wohl aber *das Werk*, das da werden soll, eine Willens-Aeuszerung noethig macht? wenn also der Unterschied zwischen Wollen and Vollbringeu keine beschraenkende Auffassung des goettlichen Seins, vielmehr durch die goettlich gewollte Beschraenktheit des geschoepflichen Seins gefordert, als goettliche Selbst beschraenkung gesetzt waere, auf Unvollkommenheit nur des Geschaffenen, nicht des Schoepfers hinwiese? Die Schoepfung ist einmal das nicht unmittelbar, was sie sein soll, sie musz es erst werden: Aufang and Ende, Weg und Ziel treten hier anseinander, das goettlich bestimmte Ergebnis haengt ab in seinem Zustande kommen von der Reihenfolge mannigfaltiger Bedingungen und Vermittlungen. Anders aber ist es im goettlichen Rathschlusse: dieser steht unmittelbar auf das Ergebnis, und nur um deswillen, in und mit ihm, bedinght von ihm send auch die Vermittlungen, Aufang and Ende sind hier zumal gesetzt. Und hiernach verhaelt sich in der That die Schoepfung zum Willen Gottes auf aehnliche Weiss, wie die aeuszere Welt zur inneren, zur menschlichen Gedankenwelt: anders folgen sich ja bei uns die Denkbestimmungen, worin ein Plan fertig wird, anders die Thaetigkeiten, wodurch wie nach gegebener, nicht frei gesetzter

---

1. By a fixed law we understand that a course is laid out, and that things follow in that course. Consequently, a law of nature in a scientific sense is nothing but an invariable order of events or sequences. As such it can effect nothing. It is the inlaid forces of nature which produce results, not its laws. For instance, the law of gravitation is frequently spoken of as producing a vast variety of results. But what is this law of gravitation? It simply denotes a certain order in which material things fall to a common centre, in certain ratios, dependent on their bulk and distance. Thus, the law of gravitation, like all the other laws of nature, effects nothing; for it

For the verb BARA (to create) according to the analogy of Scripture has but one meaning, that of *"origination, an absolute creation."* (1) This statement may appear startling to all such as are accustomed to attach every imaginable latitude of interpretation to the language of the Scriptures. Yet, a careful examination of the Hebrew Bible reveals the fact, that whenever the verb BARA (to create) is used, a

---

Ordnung ihn ausfuhren. Wenn aber jenes Ineinander von Willensbe-stimmungen, wie es im goettlichen Rathschlusse liegt, nicht unmittelbar das Weltall hervorbringt, sondern erst auseinander gelegt werden musz zu seiner zeitlichen Verwirklichung in vorangehenden und nach folgenden, in begrundenden and begrundeten Thatsachen: wie koennte diese goett-liche Selbstvermittlung, wodurch die Schoepfung so, wie sie ist, geworden ist, treffender bezeichnet werden, denn als Willens-Ausdruck, Sprechen Gottes, Machtwort and Reihe von Machtworten? Oder wenn as hiesze, nicht, Gott *sprach* sondern: er *wollte*, und es geschah, wurde so nicht das viel schlimmere Misverstaendnis nahe gelegt, ihm entstehe sein Plan erst an seinem Werke, es liege diesem kein allumfassender Rathschlusze zu Grunde? So haben wir in der biblischen Lehre vom schoepferischen

is the force of gravitation, not its law, which produces the various results which we behold.—*The Author.*

"We hear much of the 'reign of law,' and 'laws of nature.' What, however, is law, but God's ordinary modes of determining certain relations, as they have been observed by man? Philologists can trace a uniformity in the interchange of consonants in the languages of the Indo-European family, called from its discoverer 'Grimm's Law.' Words seemingly bearing no resemblance to each other are found by the application of the formula which they give, to be actually the same, as we pass from the Greek and Latin to the German, and from the German to the English. The principle recurs so frequently that it is called a 'Law,' even though the exceptions be provokingly numerous. The 'reign of law' cannot force the results, and

---

1. "Whether it be true or not that we cannot conceive the quantity of existence to be increased or diminished, there is at any rate no such inability as regards the *quantity of matter*. It may be true as a fact that no material atom has been added to the world since the Creation; but the assertion, however true, is certainly not necessary. The power which created once must be conceived as able to create again, whether that ability

new feature and addition to creation is affixed. (2) For instance we are informed that in the creative week itself, "God created great sea-monsters, and every living creature that moveth;" (3) that "God created man in His own image   *   *   male and female created He them;" (4) that He "rested from all His work which God created and made."

Sprechen Gottes einerseits die bestimmteste Ruckweisung auf den zum voraus festen Schoepferwillen, den in sich schon das gauze Werk beschliesz-enden Schoepfergedanken; anderseits ist keine Form, worin der Mensch sein Inneres Kundgibt, so gedankenmaesig und zugleich so rein durch die eigene Natur vermittelt, so muhelos verwandbar, keine so wie die mensch-liche Rede zum Gleichnis geeignet fur die allerdings auch unmittelbar werkthaetige Selbstdarstellung des goettlichen Schoepferwillens."—*Die Grundwahrheiten des biblischen Christenthums, von Ernst Woerner. p. 73-75. Theology of the Old Testament, by Dr. G. F. Oehler and Prof. G. E. Day, D. D. p. 115-118.*

---

we are made to feel that, back of it, is a more profound truth which we can-not discover after all our tentative hypotheses. Sufficient 'law' becomes manifest to exclude the idea of chance, and to show that an intelligent Will controls all that occurs beneath man's freedom. But the mysteries of that Will, man cannot always read. We must see objects from the same plane as that of Infinite Wisdom in order to discern them in all their relations, and to trace the workings of Eternal Thought concerning them. Whatever revelation God has given in his Word is simply a confession that Infinite Wisdom, in its great condescension, has made concerning itself and the whole field which it surveys, to finite man as he stands embarrassed amidst the confusion of his contracted surroundings."—*The Lutheran*, September 4th, 1890.

---

is actually exercised or not. The same conclusion is still more evident when we proceed from the consideration of matter to that of mind. Of matter, we maintain that the creation of new portions is *perfectly conceiv-able*—as a result, at least, if not as a process; of mind, we believe that such creation actually takes place. Every man who comes into the world, comes

---

2. The Hebrew word "BARA must therefore here mean origina-tion. Even in Gen. 1:21, where *bara* is employed in regard to the production of *living creatures*, we have the origination of something new: for *vitality*.

(ASAH). (5) This is not only true of the material and vital use of the word, but also in the moral and spiritual sense. When the Psalmist says "create in me a clean heart, O God;" (6) "A people which shall be created shall praise the Lord;" (7) "Thou sendest forth thy Spirit, they are created; and thou renewest the face of the earth." (1) "They are created now, and not from old;" (2) "For, behold, I create new heavens and a new earth; and the former things shall not be remembered, nor come into mind. But be ye glad and rejoice forever in that which I create; for, behold, I create Jerusalem a rejoicing, and her people a joy." (3) It is an interpretation which is endorsed by such distinguished critics as Parkhurst, Clark, Lange, Delitzsch and others who "assert that BARA means to originate *de novo*, to create in an absolute sense; and that ASAH and YETSER strictly mean to fashion out of pre-existent materials." (4)

---

into it as a distinct individual, having a personality and consciousness of his own, and that personality is a distinct accession to the number of per_ sons previously existing.   *   *   Every new person that comes into the world is a *new existence.*"—*Hamilton's Prolegomena, by Mansel, p. 267-269. Metaphysics, by Borden P. Bowne,* pp. 273-304.

sensitivity, perception are not properties of matter, neither can they be educ- ed from any organization of matter." "Gen. 1:27, 'so God created (BARA) man in *His own* image,' refers to the spiritual nature of man which alone can bear the 'image of God' and must mean origination. Gen. 2:7, 'And the Lord God formed (ASAH) man out of the dust of the earth,' refers solely to the body of man. This distinction can scarcely be accidental."—*The Theistic Conception of the World, by B. F. Cocker, D. D.* pp. 57-58. *Hours With the Bible, by C. Geikie, D. D. Vol. I.* p. 18.
  3. *Gen.* 1:21. 4. *Gen.* 1:27; 5:1, 2. 5. *Gen.* 2:3. 6. *Ps.* 51:10. 7. *Ps.* 102:18.

---

  1. *Ps.* 104:30. 2. *Isa.* 48:7. 3. *Isa.* 65:17, 18.
  4. "Creation was the absolutely free act of God, unconditioned by any pre-existing thing. Matter with its properties and forms, its temporal,

But to what part of creation does the verb BARA refer?
We reply, to the constituent elements—essence of the substances alone, all of which were spoken into existence at
"the beginning" "by the word of God," (1) when "the
foundation" (2) of the earth were laid. (3) This is also
"held by many of the best authorities who hold that the
particle AYTH means 'the very substance of,' 'the very or
real essence.' Furst, in his recently published Hebrew and
Chaldae Lexicon, gives 'being, essence, substance,' as the
meaning of '*Ayth*.' Gesenius, in his Hebrew Grammar says,
'*Ayth*' means 'being, substance.' And furthermore, he says
'*Ayth*' is a substantive derived from a pronominal stem, and
signifies essence, substance, being.' 'The particle *Ayth*' says
Aben Ezra, 'signifies the substance of a thing.' Kimchi, in
his famous 'Book of Hebrew Roots' gives a similar definition.
In the Syriac version, '*Yoth*' takes the place of '*Ayth*,' and
is very appropriately rendered in Walton's Polyglot '*esse
coeli et esse terrae*'—the being or substance of the heavens
and the earth. It is not, therefore, a fanciful   *   *
reading of this opening sentence of Divine revelation which
the Christian idea of God, and of His relation to the world,
seems to demand—'*In the beginning God originated, brought,*

---

spatial, and numerical relations; Spirit with its life and feeling, its ideas and
laws—these had all their origin in the creative Word of God. Whatever
is, and is not God, is the creature of God. This is the Biblical conception of
Creation."—*The Theistic Coneception of the World. p. 97.*

---

1. *Hebr.* 11:3.   2.   *Ps.* 102:25; *Isa.* 48:13, ff.   3 *Neh.* 9:6.

into being, the primordeal elements (1) *of the heavens and the earth.*" (2)

The reader will find no difficulty in accepting the foregoing interpretation, have no occasion to discredit the truths of the facts which are here recorded by the hand of Inspiration, confirmed by the analogy of Scripture, and endorsed by such eminent critics as the above. For the ultimate molecules (3) of matter are made, manufactured, and bear the manufacturer's brand indelibly stamped upon each of them. We shall cite the words of one whose name will ensure respect from all scientists—Prof. James Clerk Maxwell, in his lecture before the British Association as given in the *Scientific American* and cited in the *Interior*:

"Professor Clerk Maxwell lately delivered an interesting lecture before the British Association upon Molecules, by

---

1. Thus far science has hardly discovered a substance upon the planets of our solar system which cannot be matched here.—*The Author.*

2. "Dynamical Geology, Astronomical Palaetiology, Cosmogony, Molecular Physics, Abstract Dynamics, have all landed in the same inevitable conclusion that 'the existing order of things had a beginning.' * * The present order of things has not been evolved through infinite past time by the agency of laws now at work, but must have had a *distinctive beginning*, a state beyond which we are totally unable to penetrate—a state which must have been produced by other than the now acting causes.' "—*Theistic Conception of the World, by Dr. B. F. Cocker, p.* 108. *Die Naturkrafte in ihrer Wechselbeziehung, von A. Fick, p.* 87.

3. Matter presents "the essential characteristics at once of a *manufactured article* and a subordinate agent." "This precludes the idea of its being eternal and self-existent. * * It must have been created."—*Sir John Herschel's Natural Philosophy,* § 28. *Prof. Maxwell's Lecture on Molecules. Vol. VIII. p.* 441.

Lange has shown how the atom itself eludes entirely the grasp of the senses. The individual atom, which should be the ultimate constituent of matter, has no existence. "It is itself composed of sub-atoms; and these sub-atoms? They either resolve themselves into mere force-centres, or if

which is meant the subdivision of matter into the greatest possible number of portions, similar to each other.   Thus, if a number of molecules of water are combined, they form a mass of water.   Molecules of some compound substances may be subdivided into their component substances.   Thus the molecule of water separates into two molecules of hydrogen and one of oxygen.

"Professor Maxwell has calculated the size and weight of hydrogen molecules, and finds that about two millions of them, placed side by side in a row, would occupy a length of about one twenty-fifth of an inch, and that a package of them, containing a million, million, million, million of them, would weigh sixty-two grains, or not quite one-eighth of an ounce.

"Each molecule throughout the universe, bears impressed on it the stamp of a metric system as distinctly as does the meter of the archives of Paris, or the double royal cubit of the Temple of Karnac.

"No theory of evolution can be formed to account for the similarity of molecules, for evolution necessarily implies continuous change, and the molecule is incapable of growth or decay, of generation and destruction.   None of the processes of nature, since the time when nature began, have produced the slightest difference in the properties of any molecule.   We are therefore unable to ascribe either the

---

in them again elastic impact has to play any part, they must in turn consist of sub-atoms, and we shall again have that process running on into infinity.
    *   *   Accordingly there is already contained in Atomism itself, while it seems to establish Materialism, the principles which break up all matter, and thus cut away the ground from Materialism also."—*History of Materialism by Lange, Lichtenberger, Vol. II, p.* 376.

existence of the molecules or the identity of their properties to the operation of the causes which we call natural. On the other hand, the exact equality of each molecule to all others of the same kind gives it, as Sir John Herschel has well said, the essential character of a manufactured article, and precludes the idea of its being eternal and self-existent.

"Thus we have been led, along a strictly scientific path, very near to the point at which science must stop. Not that science is debarred from studying the internal mechanism of a molecule which she cannot take to pieces, any more than from investigating an organism which she cannot put together, but in tracing back the history of matter, science is arrested when she assures herself, on the one hand, that the molecule has been made, and on the other that it has not been made by any of the processes we call natural. (1)

"Science is incompetent to reason upon the creation of matter itself out of nothing. We have reached the utmost

---

1. "The physical universe has, perhaps, no more general characteristic than this,—its laws are mathematical relations. * * If we are to give any credit to science, there can be no doubt about the weights and measures and numbers. This question, then, is alone left. Could anything else than intelligence thus weigh, measure, and number? Could mere matter know the abstrusest properties of space and time and number, so as to obey them in the wondrous way it does? Could what has taken so much mathematical knowledge and research to apprehend, have originated with what was wholly ignorant of all quantitative relations? * * The belief in a Divine Creator is alone capable of rendering rational the fact that mathematical truths are realized in the material world."—*Theism, by Robert Flint, pp.* 136-137.

"Wurtz's learned book upon the Atomic Theory sufficiently shows how far the ultimate particles of matter are governed in all their combinations by invariable laws. The theory or hypothesis of chemical atoms, of which Dalton was the originator, and which Wurtz has developed and confirmed by his extensive and conclusive researches, represents compound bodies as formed by the grouping of atoms in fixed number, and possessing weights

limit of our thinking faculties when we have admitted that because matter cannot be eternal and self-existent, it must have been created. It is only when we contemplate, not matter in itself, but the form in which it actually exists, that our mind finds something on which it can lay hold. That matter, as such, should have certain fundamental properties, that it should exist in space and be capable of motion, that its motion should be persistent, and so on, are truths which may, for anything we know, be of the kind which metaphysicians call necessary. We may use our knowledge of such truth for purposes of deduction, but we have no data for speculating as to their origin.

"But that there should be exactly so much matter and no more in every molecule of hydrogen, is a fact of a very diffierent order. We have here a particular distribution of matter, a collocation, to use the expression of Dr. Chalmer's, of things which we have no difficulty in imagining to have

---

fixed by Dalton, were true proportional numbers; they represented the proportions according to which bodies combine, and which are expressed by the relative weights of their smaller particles. We there obtain a true atomic notation. Atomicity is distinguished from affinity, in that it expresses the saturating capacity of atoms as a property inherent in their nature, while 'affinity is the force of combination, the chemical energy determining the intensity and the direction of chemical reactions.' The deductions as to the nature of matter itself which M. Wurtz draws from the atomic theory, are of great interest; 'Atoms,' he says, 'are not material points; they possess a sensible dimension, and doubtless a fixed form; they differ in their relative weights and in the motions with which they are animated. They are indestructible and indivisible by physical and chemical forces, for which they act, in some manner, as points of application. The diversity of matter results from the primordial differences, perpetually existing in the very essence of these atoms, and in the qualities which are the manifestation of them. Atoms attract each other, and thus atomic attraction is affinity. It is doubtless a form of universal attraction, but it differs from it in that, if it is obedient to the influence of mass, it depends

been arranged otherwise. The form and dimensions of the orbits of the planets, for instance, are not determined by any law of nature, but depend upon a particular collocation of matter. The same is the case with respect to the size of the earth, from which the standard of what is called the metrical system has been derived. But these astronomical and terrestrial magnitudes are far inferior in scientific importance to that most fundamental of all standards which forms the basis of the molecule system.

"Natural causes, as we know, are at work, which tend to modify, if they do not at length destroy, all the arrange ments and dimensions of the earth and the whole solar system. But though in the course of ages catastrophies have occurred, and may yet occur in the heavens; though ancient systems may be dissolved and new systems evolved out of their ruins; the molecules out of which these systems are built—the foundation stones of the material universe—remain

---

also on the quality of the atoms. Affinity is elective, as has been said for a hundred years. It gives rise to aggregations of atoms, to molecules and chemical combinations. In the latter, the atoms are no longer free in their motions; they execute their motions in a kind of co-ordinated manner, and constitute a system in which everything is solid and in which they are under control" (pp. 308, 309). Wurtz refers to Hemholtz's experiments and Thomson's speculations as to the vortex motions which would exist in a perfect fluid free from all friction. * * A fluid fills all space, and what we call matter are portions of this fluid which are animated with vortex motion. There are innumerable legions of very small fractions or portions, but each of these portions is perfectly limited, distinct from the entire mass, and distinct from all others, not only in its own substance, but in its mass and its mode of motion—qualities which it will preserve for ever. These portions are atoms. In the perfect medium which contains them all, none of them can change or disappear, none of them can be formed spontaneously. Everywhere atoms of the same kind are constituted after the same fashion and are endowed with the same properties. (pp. 328, 329)"—*A Study of Origins, by Ed. De Pressense, D. D. pp.* 144, 145.

unbroken and unworn. They continue this day as they were created, perfect in number, and measure, and weight, and form the ineffacable characters impressed on them we may learn that those aspirations after accuracy in measurement, truth in statement, and justice in action, which we reckon among our noblest attributes as men, are ours because they are essentially constituents of the image of Him who in the beginning created, not only the heavens and the earth, but the materials of which the heavens and the earth consist." (1)

The last word of science on this subject was spoken by Dr. Siemens in his Inaugural Address as President of the British Association for the Advancement of Science, in which, after an able review of the progress of the arts and sciences during the year, he concluded with a reverent doxology to the God who made this progress conduce to the welfare of mankind. He concludes:

"We shall thus find that in the great workshop of nature there are no laws of demarcation to be drawn between the most exalted speculation and commonplace practice, and that all knowledge must lead up to one great result—that of an intelligent recognition of the Creator through His works. So then, we, members of the British Association, and fellow-workers in every branch of science, may exhort one another in the words of the American bard who has so lately departed from among us:

> 'Let us then be up and doing,
> With a heart for any fate;
> Still achieving, still pursuing,
> Learn to labor and to wait.' "

---

1. *Errors of Evolution, etc., by Robert Patterson*, p. 74-76.

Thus true science contradicts the Nebular Hypothesis as unproven and incapable of proof; as contradicted by all the arrangements of our solar system; as contrary to the first principles of mechanics; as assuming an eternal homogeneous matter which has no existence in heaven or in earth; and as contrary to the fundamental constitution of the molecules of matter; in a word as an impossible dream. The atheistic notion of an eternal or self-creating world, is thus seen to be utterly unscientific and absurd. We fall back upon the sublime declaration of the Bible, "In the beginning" on the first instant of time "God created" instantaneously, out of nothing *outside* of Himself, the very substance in essentia of "the heavens and the earth." (1)

Let us examine some of the solids that are contained in the crust of the earth, and behold the wonders contained therein. Of the seventy "substances which refuse further solution by processes at present known to us, are considered elemental; *   *   that these elements are as distinctly marked, in their character, in the total solar and sideral systems as with us on the earth.

"As the physical problem actually stands, we find the elements of matter will combine together and form new substances as unique in character as the elements themselves; as, for instance, the gas hydrogen and the gas oxygen combined form water a substance whose properties are as definitely marked as are those of its constituents. The gas oxygen will combine with solid carbon, as coal, and both will disappear

---

1. *Errors of Evolution, by Robert Patterson, p. 76-77.*

in new compounds having properties utterly unlike their potencies to those of either of their constituents. It is with these compounds that we usually deal on this earth, and they are what we commonly designate as 'matter.' There are very few elements which we find in a pure state. The crust of the earth, so far as we have observed it, is made up predominantly of chemical compounds. The water, and the bases of soils, and the rocks, are compounds. But the significant thing about all these compounds is that in them *their elements co-exist always in exact mathimatical ratios.* The law of definite proportions is one of the first and of the last truths of chemistry.

"So exact are the combinations of the elements, that you could make a book account, if you chose, of the chemistry of matter, in this way for instance:—

One Molecule Water,

		Dr.
To	Hydrogen Atoms	2
To	Oxygen Atoms	1

And that account will stand good for any aggregate of the molecules of water in the sea, air and universe. If you took for examination the common salt out of the water of the sea, your book account would run:—

One Molecule Salt,

		Dr.
To	Chlorine Atoms	1
To	Sodium Atoms	1

And that account will stand good for all the salt of sea and air.   *   *   A slate carries in its composition the following formula, or an equally intricate:—

$$
\text{Slate}
\begin{cases}
\text{Silica} = Si\ O_2 \\
\text{Iron Oxide} = Fe_2\ O_3 \\
\text{Alumina} = Al_2\ O_3 \\
\text{Potash} = K_2\ O \\
\text{Magnesia} = Mg\ O
\end{cases}
H_2\ O
$$

"The varieties of slate are made by differing mixtures of the constituent minerals in the above formula.   *   *
Take a piece of granite. You have dead matter there surely enough, *Ne plus ultra.* When you strike granite, the geologist tells you, you have come to azoic matter. But granite may be said metaphorically to be *alive* with the mathematical expressions of intelligence. It is peculiarly alive with such thought. If I write out a formula for granite, it would stand like this, for one variety:—

Granite
- Quartz = $Si\ O_2$
- Feldspar =
  - $Si\ O_2$
  - $Al_2\ O_3$
  - $K_2\ O$
  - $Fe_2\ O_3$
- Mica =
  - $Si\ O_2$
  - $Al_2\ O_3$
  - $Mg\ O$
  - $Fe_2\ O_3$

"So far as any of the constituent minerals are hydrated. $H_2\ O$ is to be added to its symbol. The different varieties of granite will be found by varying quantities of quartz, feldspar, and mica, or by replacing mica with horublands, or, in one mode, by substituting for potash of feldspar, soda or lime. But, whatever the variety of granite, its formula is registered in definite arithmetic.

"Now the amount of this arithematical reckoning in this matter of the *earth* is so stupendous that we may call it infinite. Think of the number of chemically combined molecules in the granite, in the sandstone, limestones, ores and clay! Every atom of every molecule in all this mass of matter is numbered and definitely yoked with its fellow and fellows.   *   *   We have not yet arrived at the point

where chemical compounds are detected or identified on the sun, or the stars, or in comets. But, as meteors sometimes bring us a chemical composition at least as complicated as granite; and as the evidence points to the formation of that composition outside our atmosphere; and as we have found many of the elements, in the heavenly bodies, with which we are here familiar; and as they there exhibit similar deportment as with us, and manifest like potencies,—we are justified in concluding that chemical combination has taken place, and will take place, in the same manner elsewhere as here.   *   *   There is an *Erdgeist* or a greater *Stoffgeist*
    Working and weaving in endless motion
    An infinite ocean
of testimony to an Infinite Intelligence—that too in the present tense—for the universe is yet young and we are beholding it making. 'My Father worketh up to this time' is the profoundest present truth." (1)

To what wonderful mysteries does organized matter testify? The most diverse substances in form, color and odor are the product of elements which their Creator alone could harmonize and combine in tangible forms; and all are infimitesimal particles of the works of God—a truth which none will doubt but such as refuse to be enlightened by His Holy Spirit, or to learn from the book of nature—the temple of the universal Architect. Who created all the elements of all the matter that fills the Universe! Who stored away in the great earth-laboratory what has proven to be the halo of our

---

1. *The Intellectual Elements in Matter, by Rev. Chas. C. Boulder, in* "*Bibleotheca Sacra," July* 1889, p. 129—436.

favored planet! Had it not been for the creation of these elements or framers at "the beginning" of the first instant of time, there would have been no cosmical fire, no molten masses, no secret laboratories out of which all the systems and suns and stars of the Universe were to be born.   It is a conception of ours which we shall endeavor to develop and simplify throughout the following pages, and which the thoughtful student will discover to be not a novelty in theory but a profound truth which is expressed in the ancient Hebrew language, endorsed by the Mythology of the ancient nations, witnessed by the different strata of the various epochs through which our planet passed, and will be welcomed as hints by the thinkers among the Chemists and Geologists, Astronomers and Theologians.   Consequently, we would suggest to the presumptuously wise, not to pass judgment on these pages before they have been carefully read, and above and beyond everything, not to judge hastily the works and word of God, for by so doing they assume a perfect knowledge of Him who is the Author of both, how he should have constituted and governed His own universe.

CHAPTER III.

THE ORIGIN OF THE UNIVERSE.

GEN. I : 2.

"*And* (1) *the earth was waste*," (Heb. THOHU—desolateness) "*and void*" (Heb. BOHU—emptiness) "*and darkness was upon the face*" (Heb. PHANA—countenance, face, surface) "*of the deep*" (Heb. THEHOM —depth) of the cosmical system on high around the earth; "*and the Spirit*" (Heb. RUACH) (2) "*of God moved*" (Heb. MERACHEPHETH—was brooding upon, hovered over)—dwelled on high "*upon the face of the waters*," (Heb. MAYIM)—vapors and aqueous matter that encompassed the systems, suns, and stars.

There is a gospel in the Universe which when compared with the earth and the earth contrasted with our known solar system, will go far toward explaining many of the

---

1. The second verse here is linked on to the first by a *copulative* conjunction, which is used as a *link* at the beginning of all the verses narrating creative acts. Thus we have *a chain of facts not broken*, but linked one to

2. The Hebrew word RUACH here means "the Spirit of God" and not the *wind*, for there could not have been any wind when there was as yet no air and no "firmament of the earth." In fact, we are first told in Gen. 8:1,

seeming mysteries and perplexing questions that confront
the Christian and Philosopher in the creative week.   While
God's action and method of working in the Universe is a
continuous expression of thought, and a revelation of a plan
which is manifest in all that space and time bound—which
is but the realization of a plan of perfect and absolute reason,
yet we must be careful not to Deify reason here or elsewhere;
for "St. Austin accurately says 'we *know* what rests upon
reason; we *believe* what rests upon *authority*.   But reason
itself must rest at last upon authority; for the original data
of reason do not rest upon reason, but are necessarily of
what is beyond itself.   These data are, therefore, in rigid
propriety *beliefs* or *trusts*.   Thus it is, that the last reason,
we must, perforce philosophically admit, that *belief* is the
primary condition of reason, and not reason the ultimate
ground of *belief*.   We are compelled to surrender the proud
Intellige ut credas of Abelard, to content ourselves with the
humble *Crede ut intelligas* of Anselm,"   (1)

---

the other. The copulative VAV means a *hook;* and is used to connect words,
to hook sentences one to another.—*The Author*.

after the Deluge, that "God made a wind to pass over the earth" which
brought sunshine and rain, affected the different zones, and established the
course of the trade-winds and the gulf-streams of to-day.—*The Author*.

---

1. *Sir Wm. Hamilton in Reed's Works, as quoted in "A Vocabulary of the
Philosophical Sciences," by C. P. Krauth, D. D., LL. D.   p. 65.*

· That the reason and mind of man could not have understood God, terrestrially or celestially, nor the design of His works, natural or spiritual, is
evident from the very fact that God was obliged personally to address and
reveal Himself unto the patriarchs and the prophets of the Old Testament,
and in the fullness of time to send and speak unto mankind through His
Son Jesus Christ.—*The Author*.

What a wonderful harmony and proof of the Divine origin and authority of the Scriptures do we discover in not only the languages which it uses, the history which it records, the doctrines which it advocates, and the life which it reveals; but also here, when we compare the verse under consideration with what the apostle St. Paul records of the same event several thousand years later! He says "By faith we understand" (Literal—we perceive) "that the worlds have been framed" (Literal—adjusted) "by the word of God, so that what is seen hath not been made out of things which do appear" (Literal—not out of things appearing). (1)

Thus was the Universe ushered into existence—the substance of the reality of matter,—another stage "marked by the development of some new idea in the system of progress." (2) And to which this earth of ours also, now desolateness and emptiness belongs, and whose condition here can well be likened to the condition of the moon to-day. But of what significance was the "darkness" on high, surrounding the then already moving earth on every side? Was it not the Universe of systems, and suns, and stars;—this the great "deep," the "thick darkness." (3) the "heavens of heavens," (4) here wrapped in the blackness of darkness, because "light" had not yet been created; (5) the properties of the elements of the "firmament" intended for the earth between the "waters which were *under* the firmament from the

---

1. *Heb.* 11:3. *Ps.* 33:6.
2. *Manuel of Geology, by James D. Dana, LL. D.* p. 137, 3d Ed.
3. *Job* 38:9. 4. *Ps.* 148:4. 5. *Gen.* 1:3; *Jer.* 4:3.

waters which were *above* the firmament" had not yet been adjusted; (1) the aqueous masses of matter and the vapors that moved around the sun and the planets of our solar system; the dense aqueous matter, mineral and metal-rings that encompassed the "waste and void" earth had not yet been lifted or dispersed.

That the Universe of worlds did not come "from nothing," (2) was not in a "chaotic condition," nor a creation of "inactivity," is evident from the fact that nowhere in the Universe is nothing found, nor a state of confusion known, (3) nor a stage of inactivity discernible. Consequently, to speak of the infinity of space and time is equally as absurd; for all those who assert this, affirm that in order to obtain a centre of gravity, to become a centre of attraction, this can be accomplished or is possible *without* boundaries to our Universe and system; and at the same time they ignore the order of things therein successive. (4) Everywhere and in

---

1. *Gen.* 1: 6, 7.

2. "The question of *absolute* creation has been prejudiced by the persistent employment of the old formula of 'creation out of nothing,' as though (nothing) contained the cause of existence, and the universe was developed out of nothing. The Christian Fathers, who first employed the phrase *ktisis ek tou me ontos*, never indulged in such representations. The idea they sought to express was that the production of (*otherness*), the awarding of existence to something besides Himself, was an absolutely free act of God which was not conditioned by anything external to Himself—in a word, that God is the positive original ground of all existence."—*Theistic Conception of the World*, p. 92.

3. If there was chaos in the beginning, there must be chaos now. God is not a God of confusion.—*The Author.*

4. "In what manner is the doctrine of the absolute creation of the world by God implied in Scripture? 1st—In all those passages that teach that God is an absolute Sovereign, and that the creature is *absolutely* de-

everything do we discover the power, wisdom and benefi-
cence of a living and ever active God, who is the Creator
and Originator of all power, all force, all energies. This
cannot be otherwise: for action is the logic (1) of reason,
reason is the logic of thought, thought is the logic of mind.
mind is the logic of life, life is the logic of the God-life.—
The personal God, Who left *His imprint of wholeness,—com-
pleteness and of perfection*, even on our solar system in its
earliest stage of development; and this by the law of *circularity.*   (2) "The circle is the archetype of all forms, physi-
cally as well as mathematically. It is the most complete

---

pendent on him, 'in whom we live and move and have our being'—Acts 17:
28; Neh. 9:6; Col. 1:16; Rev. 4:11; Rom. 11:36; 1 Cor. 8:6. Now it is evident
that if the essences and primordial principles of all things are not immediately created by God out of nothing, but are eternally self-existent inde-
pendently of Him, then He, in His office of Creator and Providential Gov-
ernor of all things, must be conditioned and limited by the pre-existing
essential properties and powers of those primordial elements. In which case
God would not be absolutely Sovereign, nor the things made absolutely dependent upon His will.

2d In all those passages which teach that the Kosmos, the 'all things,'
had a beginning,   Ps. 102; John 17:5, 24."—*Outlines of Theology, by A. A.
Hodge, D. D., p. 240.*

---

1. The term *logic* is here used not in its relation to reason: but rather in
the sense in which design is the expression of Mind.—*The Author.*

2. "That there are in the activities of nature central and circular actions is evidenced by innumerable instances both in organic and inorganic
productions, and in the actions and movements of the heavenly
bodies. By central actions are meant such actions as commence in, or
act from, a central point, and extend action or energizing power outward.
By circular action is meant any rounding or circular action that produces
round forms, or circular motion, or motion that returns through any
circuitous route to its source: or where dependent and reciprocal actions
are necessary to complete a cycle or continue an activity.

figure, the most stable under violence, the most economical of material; its proportions are the most perfect and harmonious; and therefore it admits of the utmost variety consistent with unity of effect. The universe has apparently been framed according to this type. Nature attains her ends, not in a series of straight lines, but in a series of circles; not in the utmost direct, but in the most round-about

---

"Concretions are formed on a central point, or nucleus, around which concentric layers are gathered from matter in a state of fusion or solution. The rounded balls or boulders so abundantly found in some large masses of igneous rock formations show that there must have been innumerable centers of consolidation around which layer upon layer of fused matter cooled and hardened.

"Nodular spathic iron ore, and many rounded concretions, are instances where matter in solution aggregated around a central point.

"There are centers of action, repelling and attractive, indicated and manifested in the minutest particles of matter. Heat forms repelling centers that expand and separate material substances, that in some instances cohesion seems to be almost entirely destroyed. Bubbles in water are round, and water separates into globules. Granulation shows central actions and in many substances produces rounded forms. There are storm centers in the atmosphere and circling actions in the oceans.

"Gravity, one of the universal and all-prevading forces of nature, seems to be drawing matter from all directions towards a common center, and this common center seems to be the center of the earth; and no doubt this force has a centralizing action wherever its influence can be made effective, even in minute particles of matter.

"Vital force in all its incipient actions commences in minute central points, forms spheres, and develops them into cells of living matter, from which plants and animals are organized in accordance with the particular forms of the vital energy.

"In animal life, especially in the human family, are vital and mental centers of action and circulating movements. The heart sends the blood through all parts of the body and keeps up its propelling action so that the blood is forced to move in an apparently continuous circuit. The brain is the center of mental action, the great storehouse of knowledge where information is received and knowledge stored. It is the little central dynamo from which the intellectual energy of man transmits energizing, directing and controlling power throughout the body, and compels the physical powers, and even other forces of nature, to be its subservient agencies. It

way.   All her objects, organic and inorganic, have a tendency to assume the circular form, and in the attainment of
this form consists their highest perfection.   *   *
And as our eyes behold the effects of this law in moulding
the forms in nature, so our minds furnish us with evidences

---

utilizes impressions received through the senses, converts them into knowledge, and makes this knowledge the power through which it acquires dominion over matter and life and over the forces of nature.

"The renewal, or reproduction, of life, vegetable and animal, is a cyclic
and multiplying action extending through a series of changes from seed to
seed.   So common are these wonderful cyclic actions in life that we scarcely notice the astonishing changes that take place in the development of a
seed until it reproduces its like.   It is a remarkable fact, too, that seeds of
most plants, and eggs of animals, are of a rounded form, thus showing a
universal tendency of a central and circular action in vital energy.

"Between vegetable and animal life there are many reciprocal and dependent actions, which show their close relation and connection, and here
the two form a circuit of life-giving agencies.   The wastes of one supply
the wants of the other, and rounds of reciprocal actions are the sustaining
powers of both.

"A beautiful illustration of the reciprocal dependence of vegetable and
animal life can be seen in a common aquarium.   By placing a fish in a vessel of water, the water will in a very short time become unfit for the fish to
live in, but by placing water plants with sufficient earth or stones in the
vessel, the water will be purified by the plants so that the fish can live; but
when the plants begin to die and decay, snails or worms that will eat the
decaying vegetables must be added, or the fish will die; with the snails added the water will remain pure for an almost indefinite time.   Here are a
series of actions and reactions necessary to maintain a certain condition
that will enable both vegetable and animal life to exist, which shows how
closely related and how dependent upon each other these two kingdoms of
life are, and how beautifully the law of reciprocal action between them is
balanced.   The purity of the atmosphere has been brought about and is
maintained by similar reciprocal actions between vegetable and animal
life; through the absorption of carbon by the former, which is exhaled by
the latter as a useless and dangerous substance, the purity of the atmosphere is maintained, and the circuit of actions and reactions continued.

"The earth rotates around its axis and revolves with all the planets of
the solar system around the sun as their central point; and the sun radiates
light from this central position through the whole of this system.   Here is
positive proof of central action and circular motion, and a clear indication

in the plan according to which the different parts of creation have been constructed." (1)

That our earth therefore has a globular form need not surprise us, nor that its aqueous strata enveloping it, and upon whose "circle" (Heb. CHUG—arch, vault, compass) (2) the Lord "sitteth" (2) and "walketh" (3) should be the first to descend, and thus make "this ponderous substance, heavier than iron, which constitutes the solid structure"— the "waste and void"—"of our earth, compared with which the geological strata of our earth than a coat of paint on a brick house, and which must be unlike anything with which we are acquainted;" (4) the only habitable planet of our

of reciprocal dependence; showing that in all creation there is a close relation and connection, and that while there are special centers of action, and circular and cyclical movements in the minutest particles of matter, and throughout all nature up to the forming of worlds and system of worlds, and moving the same in circular orbits through boundless space during endless time; yet in all these apparently independent bodies of matter and actions of forces there is such a close relation and reciprocal dependence as to show that all nature is one, and that all her activities are energized, brought into action and controlled by some Great Power, *whose center of action exists everywhere, and whose limiting circumference is nowhere.*

"In the movements of the heavenly bodies we have an illustration of the law of central and circular action on a scale of grandeur and magnitude that surpasses all human comprehension, and yet the same law prevails everywhere, in the minutest particle of matter as well as in a system of worlds. Evidently the general and universal forces of nature have in themselves an inherent law of central action, and of a circular, cyclical or reciprocal moving power, and that these actions and movements always produce corresponding effects and results where the conditions are favorable, or where no special forces interfere with these general actions and movements.

1. *Bible Teachings in Nature, by H. Macmillan, D. D., LL. D., p. 312-314.*
2. Isa. 40:22.｜ The Hebrew word CHUG, which means *arch, vault, com-*
3. Job 22:14. *｜pass* is used in both of these passages.
4. *Reed's Geology.*

system to this hour, more than fills us with astonishment, reverence and awe. (1) And yet, such is the case. Astronomers inform us: "Mercury is too hot to be the abode of life, the sun pouring upon it with from four to ten times the heat we have. Venus can only be habitable when she receives one-half of her present heat. All the facts about Mars indicate an intense cold, which would render life impossible. Jupiter, in addition to being a young world, not yet ready to invite inhabitants, receives but little heat from the sun, and there are signs of great hurricanes for weeks together. Saturn's rings hide the sun's rays, and throw a great part of the planet's surface in shadow. Uranus and Neptune are at such distances from the sun, whose light and heat diminish according to the square of the distance, that even the Esquimaux would find their climate more intolerable than that within an Artic circle." (2)

"The agencies of activity in nature, whether general or special, always operate from an interior or central point. The sun is the central acting agent of the solar system, and the rays of light radiating throughout this system are no doubt the causative agencies of activity in all the movements of the bodies within that system, and have much to do with all the activities that take place upon the earth.

"Without the rays of the sun this earth would be a solid body of inert matter, notwithstanding the theory that the interior of the earth is in an extremely heated condition; for without the heat produced by the sun's rays, the surface of the earth would long ago have been frozen into a solid actionless mass.

"The fact that the earth is part of the solar system and receives continually volumes of energizing power from the sun, seems to indicate very strongly that the sun receives in some form a return from the earth, and that there is reciprocal and compensating action between the two. However this may be, it is a well known fact that the sun is a great central

---

1.   According to the above facts, the prophets of Millenialism will have to reconstruct their theology.—*The Author*.

2.   *R. G. in N. Y. Observer*, 1889.

But let us return to the great primitive earth-laboratory —"swaddling-band" (1) of the "great deep" (2) of darkness moving with the "waste and void" earth in all its motions; and upon the face of which "the Spirit of God" dwelt then. and does now,—including the heart of the believing; for the Christian religion is the manifestation of the abiding of God in men's heart,—the victory of faith. In this laboratory were stored away the invisible things out of which the visible Universe, and habitable earth were to be "framed." The original matter-rings, the vaporized minerals and metals that thus encompassed the primitive earth, were to be lifted by the cosmical fire and afterwards swung from their anchorage, and gradually to sink back again toward the attracting central body, to form the strata of our present globe;—many of the later strata furnishing the environment and habitation for the vegetable and animal organisms

source of activity, and that the movement of the immense bodies of the solar system at a high velocity around this central source of activity, shows a great circular moving power: but grand and striking as this illustration of the law of central and circular action in the solar activities appears, there is in man a concentration of forces, and of laws governing their activities, that constitute a more varied and more perfect system of agencies of activity than can be found anywhere else in nature.

"In man matter, force and mind—the three elements that constitute everything manifested and indicated in nature—are united in one interacting personality. In this personality are centres of chemical action with perfect laboratories; a centre of vital action supplying the chemical centres with vital energy, and receiving in return the vitalized chemical products, and thus forming a complete circuit of reciprocal action. But at the head, and in the head, of this personality is another center of action, with an energy that permeates every part of the personality, and reaches out beyond it in every direction. It is the central sun that lights up the whole

1. *Job* 38:9. 2. *Gen.* 7:11; *Ps.* 36:6.

therein entombed, and all of them together witnessing the successive stages of the transformations through which the earth passed before it was a habitable world.

But this is not all. The vapors of the earth's "deep" were also the ocean of oceans, and the source of all waters, when the "dry land" appeared and the "seas" were formed; for the earth was originally a "ponderous substance, heavier than iron,   *   *   unlike anything with which we are acquainted," "waste and void."   It was also the remains of this belted canopy of vapors which can be likened to those which envelope Jupiter and Saturn to-day, possibly more dense, that were to give to our first parents a green-house roof and climate, where they were in need of no clothing, that favored them and their children with a great old age, permitted plants and animals to develope to a gigantic form and size in an earth that knew of no storms or rains for 1600 years, because neither the canopy surrounding the sun nor the vapors shrouding the earth had been dispelled or cleared away;—until the time when "all the fountains of the great deep were broken up and the windows of heaven

---

personality, discovers its needs and its dangers, and takes charge of it with all its surroundings and makes every provision for its needs, its safety and its comfort. It receives in return from the other parts the fullest and most perfect portion of the vitality.

"Here are distinct centres of action in a three-fold personality, all in perfect unity of action and reaction, each dependent upon the others, and all sustaining each other and making together a complet whole. In all nature there are no more and no different forces at work, and no different laws governing their actions than there are in this personality. Man is a complete world in himself—a perfect cosmos; and as a centre of activity he stands at the head of creation, as the embodiment of all the agencies of activity in the past, and as the controlling energy in the progressive development of the future."—*Isaac Hoffer.*

were opened." (1) When the *last* and outermost earth-rings
of the aqueous vapors fell to deluge the whole globe, and to
destroy all mankind, but Noah and his family, and the animals in the Ark which were again to reinhabit the air, dale,
hill and mountain. In the equatorial Zones it was a down-
rush of waters, at the poles a down-rush of snow which entombed the "Mammals" in an ocean of ice. (2) These were
"the waters which were *above* the firmament:" (3) the
"Great Abyss" of the Hebrews, the "Nilus" of the Egyptians,
and the "Oceanus" of the Greeks. After the downfall of
which God first "made a wind to pass over the earth" (4)
which brought sunshine and rain, affected the different
Zones, and established the course of the trade-winds and
gulf streams of to-day.

---

1. *Gen.* 7:11; *Ps.* 36:6.

2. That the mammals were buried in a down-rush of snow is evident
from the fact that "if they had not been frozen as soon as killed they must
quickly have decomposed by putrefaction. But this eternal frost could not
have taken possession of the region which these animals inhabited except
by the same cause which destroyed them."—*Cuvier*.

"The ice or congealed mud, in which the bodies of such quadrupeds
were enveloped, has never once been melted since the day they perished, so
as to allow the free percolation of water through the matrix; for, had this
been the case, the soft parts of the animals could not have remained un-
decomposed."—*Lyell*.

The only cause that could possibly produce what Cuvier and Lyell
truthfully state,—the immediate death and refrigeration of the Mammal
and his congeners was none other than the down-rush of waters in the now
called Torrid and Temperate Zones which deluged the continents to the
depth of the highest mountains; and the down-rush of snow at the poles
which gave birth to the "Glacial Age" of which Geology has so many wonders to tell. All this occurred in the time of the Noachian Deluge when
"all the fountains of the great deep were broken up, and the windows of
heaven were opened."—*The Author*.

3. *Gen.* 1:7.   4. *Gen.* 8:1.

CHAPTER IV.

THE APPEARANCE OF LIGHT.

GEN. 1 : 3, 4, 5.

"And God said, Let there be" a new combination of the elements to produce *"light"* (Heb. OR) (1) *"and there was light,"* a cosmical fire. *"And God saw the light,"* which now for the first time illuminated the Universe *"that it was good; and God divided"* (Heb. BEN—betwixt) *"the light"* of our solar system *"from the darkness"* (2) in the thick and dark aqueous matter-rings that enveloped the earth. *"And God called the light"* (3) that illuminated *"day, and the darkness"* that followed *"He called night."* *"And there was evening and there was morning, one day."*

A striking confirmation of what Moses records here is found in II. Cor. IV.:6, where St. Paul writes: "It is God

---

1. "The Hebrew word OR, which is used for 'light,' Gen. 1:3 appears also to comprehend 'fire' in its signification. See Isa. 44:16; 47:14; Ezek. 5:2,

2. "Light is the first *separation.* It is 'divided from darkness' 'and God called the light *day* and the darkness He called *night.*' This is God's own

3. "It is immaterial for our purpose whether, with the earliest evolutionists, we regard these changes as taking place in a relative homogeneous substance, a diffused nebula, or whether, with their later followers, we set

that said, Light shall shine out of darkness" (Literal—the God that commanded out of darkness light to shine). The Apostle here takes us back once more to the dark abyssmal depth, the great primitive laboratory of the Universe shrouded still in "thick darkness." (1) The Spirit of God that once "hovered over" the midnight "darkness" of the upper "deep," directs him to record, that it is *there* that

---

compared with verse 4."—*Genesis and Geology,.by Denis Crafton, B. A. and Prof. Ed. Hitchcock, D. D., LL. D.* p. 90.

naming, and we must take it as our guide in the interpretation of the subsequent 'days.' Obviously, it is * * the phenomenon, the appearing itself which is for the first time called day."—*Theistic Conception of the World,* p. 148.

Light not only is here the prime agent of God by which all the transformations in the earth's canopy and on the earth's surface were to be effected during the creative period; but it still is to this day the only known agent to which all kinds of motion upon and around the physical world may be traced.

Then again, how forcibly does this natural light as an agent of the first creation, whose forces effected all the extraordinary changes in the creative week and have ever since been the balancing power of the material world; recall to every Christian the spiritual light as an agent of the second creation, whose forces emanating through this "Light of the world" effected all the extraordinary changes in the history of mankind, and are ever since the balancing power of the spiritual world.—*The Author.*

them down to aggregative action in comparatively solid and discrete masses (meteors), like those which we know to exist in large tracts within the sphere of the solar system. But the important point to notice in either case is this, that these groupings and sub-groupings took place under the influence of forces, and that the potential energy of separation between the masses or molecules became kinetic as they clashed together, and assumed the form of heat. The various masses thus became each of them a sun, aggregating around their several centers, and radiating their energy into the surrounding ether."—*Force and Energy, by Grant Allen,* p. 34.

---

1. *Job* 38:9.

light (1) was to originate and to be born. "These were not fortuitous happenings that might come to something or might come to nothing, but the systematic development of a plan devised and determined before the work began. (2) and in which, therefore, every change and every movement contributed to the result intended from the first." (3) The elements originally created by God, and which were the framers of the Universe were as yet alone, laboring in darkness. And it was out of this cosmical darkness where the elementa combinations appear merely to have effected thus far solar agglomerations such as our formless and matterless —"waste and void" earth, that the "light" was to come forth. "As yet nothing had assumed definite form or character. There were the germs of worlds, but no world. There were the elements of water and air and light, while as yet there were none of these, none of the chemical combinations or mechanical unions so familiar to us now; and the various changes in nature that we know so well to-day, had not begun. There was absolutely nothing but the dark chaotic

---

1. The elements which constitute the light had no more power in themselves to create it, than has a paving stone on the street the power to produce motion. The burning of a lamp is a manifestation of the presence of ignitable matter, but which it does not manufacture. *The Author.*

2. "The nature of chemical combinations is so occult, and their power so enormous, and their recent applications in the telegraph so far reaching and astonishing, that some are ready to hope and believe that the long-sought for perpetual motion may lie hid away among them." We reply never! For then the essence of the chemistry which gave life to the elements which gave force to the combination which gave power to an electric motor would have to be self-originating, self-preserving and independent of the mechanism which gives expression to it.—*The Author.*

3. *The Creation and the Early Development of Mankind, by J. H. Chapin, Ph. D., p. 22.*

deep." (1) A stage had been reached where a change was absolutely necessary, if the oceans of elemental combinations and agglomerations were destined.

What was needed, happened. God, by the word of His command again creates. No new elements, for these were created at "the beginning;" but a new combination of the elements, the chemical action of which would be the production of "light." And it was this combination in the cosmic "deep" of darkness that caused the cosmical fire to be born;—the fire which had become necessary, first, to mould and temper the floating agglomerations revolving in the just created necessary space: and then again, to develope and complete them as rotating planets and stars moving around fixed centres. Among the *solar fires* (2) of the systems of the Universe that bound space; (3) our solar fire also—the *sun* (4) was created, to dispel and dissipate its own cloud of

---

1. *Dr. J. H. Chapin.*

2. Of the cause of this tremendous fire and of the fuel which feeds it, science is and ever will be ignorant, for God's work here and everywhere is like Himself, beyond finding out. The elements in themselves which originated the Universe—its systems and suns and stars, as well as the light which they are here bidden to produce, are only manifestations.—A symbol is not the thing itself.— *The Author.*

3. Space is as little infinite or unbounded as is the universe of matter. It is hardly reasonable that space should have a lump of matter in it, and all the rest be empty, and that to no purpose. This is one view of this subject.—If the reader desires an elaborate presentation of the different views entertained concerning *space* and *time* we would refer him to *Browne's Metaphysics pp.* 177-272; *Gillespie's Necessary Existence of God; Final Causes, by Janet.* —*The Author.*

4. See Note 1, of page 42, as quoted from "Genesis and Geology," on "light" and "fire."

elemental darkness and that of the great primitive earth-laboratory which enveloped the world; to aid by the force of its light in the further development and final completion of the yet desolate and empty earth. Whose vaporous atmosphere according to some of the most eminent authorities in Astronomy is said to have been driven at least 200,000 miles from the earth alone, to have embraced and extended far beyond the orbit of the moon. Of this new creation which gave to the Universe the cosmical fire and to our "swaddlingband"—system, the sun, it is said "it was good." Its illumination sufficiently effected the belted canopy of our earth to enable God to "divide" betwixt the illuminous light-rings that were encompassing the earth on its march toward the Edenic day; when man, the subject of two worlds, was created to represent his Creator and God upon the earth- in worship to obey Him, in love to serve Him, and in faith to confess Him as the just and holy God, whose Love expressed and personified in His Son Jesus Christ, is as wide as the Universe, as high as heaven, and as deep as hell. "And God called" this diffusion of "light" through the vaporized clouds "day." "And the darkness" that followed on the rotating earth, making a revolution from between three hours and twenty-four hours,—according to eminent astronomers—, around its axis, "He called night." Thus were the first evening and the first morning ushered into being on the first day of our becoming earth.

When the "light" born out of the cosmic "deep" became a cosmical fire, and was "divided from the darkness" of the systems which were to rotate around their respective solar fire—the sun and centre of each system; *Creations negative* from God's laboratory had first appeared. The features most striking and best delineated in this negative of "the worlds" were those of the earth's stratified aqueous matter-rings that shrouded the Bethlehem among the planets. (1) The created visible light out of the invisible original elements produced stupendous changes. So gigantic was its effect upon the dark rings nearest to the earth, which can be likened to the dark sooty matter observed in the belts of Jupiter and Saturn to-day—suspending the unconsumed carbon which encompassed it as smoke, soot, pitchy matter; that they rushed and fell in immense deposits of black carbonaceous matter and mud upon the bottoms of the fire moulds of the earth. (2) The carbonaceous mud alone having been discovered thus far by scientists in the bottom of

---

1. "The orbits of the comets, being inclined at all angles to the sun's equator, are often out of the plane of his rotation, and fly right in the face of the Nebular Theory. The moons of Uranus revolve in a direct contrary to all the other bodies, and so contrary to the Nebular Theory. The palpable difference between the luminosity of the sun and of the other bodies, is in itself a sufficient refutation of the nebular theory which would make them all out of the same materials, and by the same process, and moreover refutes the notion of their common origin by any mere mechanical law, as Newton shows: 'The same power, whether natural or supernatural, which placed the sun in the centre of the six primary

2. "Up to the present time we are ignorant, as I have already remarked, of any internal necessity—*any mechanical law of nature*—which (like the beautiful law which connects the square of the periods of revolution with the cube of the major axis) represents the above named elements—the absolute magnitude of the planets, their density, flattening at the poles, velocity of rotation, and presence or absence of moons of the order of successions of the individual planetary bodies of each group in their dependence upon distances. Although the planet which is nearest to the sun is densest,—even six or eight times denser than some of the exterior planets, Jupiter, Saturn, Uranus and Neptune—the order of succession in the case of Venus, the Earth, and Mars is very irregular. The absolute magnitudes

thousands of upheaved lakes and ponds scattered through-out Northern Europe and the United States. In hundreds of lakes and ponds that have been drained in Ohio and Michigan by the construction of canals and railroads, and also for agricultural purposes, do we find this carbonaceous mud without a sign or symptom of vegetation, and there-fore, it was not a "peat-formation" such as Geologists have erroneously been advocating.

In fact the times are coming to a point when the master minds of Geology will of necessity become eminent Astron-omers also; besides being well versed in a *system* of The-ology; for science in its last generalization must be Theology. For it is evident from what we have been told already and shall learn before the close of this great foundation subject, that both sciences, in fact all three, are so closely allied and linked together, that what is the foundation of one is the

---

planets, placed Saturn in the centre of the orbit of His five secondary plan-ets, and the earth in the centre of the moon's orbit, and, therefore, had this cause been a blind one, *without contrivance or design*, the sun would have been a body of the same kind with Saturn, Jupiter and the earth; that is, *without light and heat*. Why there is one body in our system qualified to give light and heat to all the rest, I know no reason but because the author of the system thought it convenient.'" *Errors of Evolution*, p. 35, 36.

do, generally, as Kepler has already observed, increase with the distances; but this does not hold good when the planets are considered individually. Mars is smaller than the earth; Uranus smaller than Saturn; Saturn smaller than Jupiter, and succeeds immediately to a host of planets which, on account of their smallness, are almost immeasurable. It is true the period of rotation generally increases with the distance from the sun; but it is in the case of Mars slower than in that of the Earth; and slower in Saturn than in Jupiter." "Our knowledge of the primeval ages of the world's physical history does not extend sufficiently far to allow our de-picting the present condition of things as one of development."— *Humboldt's Cosmos, Vol. III, p. 28, Vol. IV, p. 425.*

foundation of the others, what is the corner-stone of one is the corner-stone of the others, what is the key-stone of one is the key-stone of the others. Observe, how the condition of our planet becomes the standard of the condition of our system; how the development of the earth by its aqueous rings is also the development of the other planets by the descending of their rings to-day? Thus, how beautifully and strikingly does this all-comprehending material law of development in the universe and in nature, illustrate the progressive growth of God's Kingdom of righteousness and blessedness among men! Our Saviour distinctly teaches not only that His kingdom grows, but that it grows by *epochs.* "First the blade, then the ear, after that the full corn in the ear." These are the epochs in the growth of the grain; not that it grows only in these epochs, but that its continuous growth naturally manifests itself in them; similar to the gradual material development of the earth to which Moses here has reference, and of which the Astronomers to-day speak, when the other planets of our system are mentioned. Both dominions—the material and spiritual—were thus originated and are thus energized by the same all-wise, all-powerful and ever-loving God.

CHAPTER V.

THE EARTH'S CANOPY AND STRATA.

GEN. 1 : 6, 7, 8.

"*And God said, Let there be a firmament*" for the developing earth "*in the midst of*" (Literal—in between) "*the waters, and let it*"—the newly made firmament "*divide the waters*"—aqueous rings "*from the waters*"—aqueous matter-rings that encompass the earth. "*And God*" thus "*made*" (Heb. ASAH) "*the firmament.*" (Heb. RAKIYA—to stretch, to spread out) (1) which was to be the earth's; "*and*" thereby "*divided*" permanently "*the waters which were under*" (Heb. THAHATH—from below, beneath) "*the firmament*" in the mould-marked earth,—"*from the waters*" —great oceans of water and matter that floated in its

---

1. The Hebrew word RAKIYA primarily denotes something *expanded*, or *beaten out*, like a metallic plate, (Exod. 3:3; Num. 17:4. Such is the literal sense of the root from which it comes, and such, too, is the suggested sense of the Greek *stereoma*, and the Latin *firmamentum*. They denote solidity, but this belongs only to the phenomenal conception such as is also presented in the *ourano poluchalko* and *ouranosidero* of Homer." *The Six Days of Creation, etc., by Prof. Tayler Lewis, p.* 117.

strata, thick and manifold *"which were above"* (Heb. MEAL—over) *"the firmament"*—expanse of the earth : *"And it was so."* (1) *"And God called the firmament"*—expanse of air, electricity, vapors, etc. *"Heaven."* (2) *"And there was evening"*—the darkness which closed the first day, *"and there was morning"*—the light which introduced the next day, *"A second day."*

The work of creation described here is still preparatory ; and a complete inversion and explosion of the "Nebular hypothesis," past, present, and future. The prophet Isaiah informs us how God not only created the heavens (HASHA-MAYIM) of Gen. 1:1; but that He also "framed" (Heb. YATSAR—fashioned) the earth (HAARETS) of Gen. 1:1; not to remain "waste" (THOHU—desolateness) of Gen. 1:2, rather "to be inhabited." (3) In order to reach the destined end and object of the earth's creation; what does God command the elements shrouding the earth to do, and how does

---

1. "The Hebrew RAKIYA, from RAKA (to stretch, to spread out), means properly an extension, an expanse. This is the translation adopted by Benisch, Kalisch, Delitzsch, Keil and Lange. After heat and light, the next creative formation is an *atmosphere*, with its auroral light and a cloudy canopy."—*Theistic Conception of the World*, p. 153.

2. It was as though God had said: "Let there be an expanse in the midst of the vapors, and let it be a division of vapors from vapors."

3. *Isa.* 45:18.

the "light," as the agent of God, help to effect it? (1)   Job
furnishes us with the answer, when he says: "The foundations of the earth" and "the measures thereof" stored away
originally in the "circle"—encompassing rings of the earth
were finally to be fastened."   God "shut up the sea with
doors" by the agency of the light, and thus effected the
firmamental divisions, so that "a firmament in the midst of
the waters" might appear; the decreed—"set bars and
doors" which separate—*divide* the waters from the
waters," and therefore well could say: "Hitherto shalt
thou come, and no further: And here shall thy proud waves
be stayed."   Thus was "the firmament" made to "divide"
permanently "the waters which were *under* the firmament
from the waters which were *above* the firmament"- "the
clouds the garments thereof."   (2)

In the vast ocean of aqueous matter that was suspended
on high above the earth were not only the sources whence
the materials of the strata of the earth were to be derived,
but also the forces by which they were to be borne down
each at the appointed place and time; and that its revolving
vapors must have contained great stores of unconsumed
carbon (3) possibly largely the product of igneous action, is

---

1. A very homely illustration possilby of what the "light" was as a
factor in the dividing of the waters from the waters, might be the following; namely, the power of a steam engine, is the power in the heat passing
out of the fire into the water of the boiler, and expanding into steam.   *The
Author.*

2. *Job.* 38:4–11.

3. The carbon in the diamond, in coal and in limetone, is in essence the
same as the carbon in oil, in gas and in plants.   *The Author.*

evident from our knowledge of the earth's strata. And that it was covered and concealed from the action of the air ever since its descent to the earth, is also a universally accepted fact. It was when God said "Let there be a firmament in the midst of the waters," that He originated and endowed the oxygen and nitrogen of the atmosphere with the power of retaining its æriform condition under all circumstances, while the aqueous vapors enveloping the earth were subjected to great fluctuations. The submerged "peat-beds" (1) of a later period were the product of carbon falling into an ocean of oxygen. For in this form alone (Carbonic Anhydride) could it enter into the economy of the plant and become plant food. (2)

It was also in this period of the earth's history that possibly the most stupendous changes took place on its surface; besides a complete re-arrangement of its canopy. For the crystalline and volcanic rocks—granite and its associates, basalt and lava were to be formed. And the thinkers

---

1. "There are but few readers who are not aware of the fact that a black carbonaceous soil is the superficial covering of many of the northern and northwestern states,—a coating of exceedingly black, soot-like matter, —strikingly different from that of the adjacent states. Now since it is well known to geologists that all this region thus overlain was once the bed

2. "The atmosphere now contains less carbonic acid than it did at the beginning of the Carboniferous period, by the amount stored away in the coal of the globe." And which original carbonic acid must have been considerably diminished in quantity by the time the animals were created; for the same high authority says: "Much more carbonic acid" than now exists in the atmosphere "would be injurious to animal life."—*Dana, in his Manual, p.* 340-353.

"The great element of nature is oxygen. It forms one-fifth of the volume of the atmosphere. It composes between one-half and one-third of the crust of the globe. It makes up eight-ninths of all the earth's water.

among the scientists will agree and say, that this was alone possible by deposits; because of their uniform thickness throughout the crust of the globe. (1) Yet, what have these deposits to do with the above formations of the crystalline and volcanic rocks—granite and its associates, basalt and lava, the deposits of the Lawrentian period alone closing the Archaean Age, being 30,000 feet in thickness or depth in parts of America. What has the sand-stone, lime-stone and shale, the "old red sand-stone" of the Devanian age to do with the crystallization and formation of these strata, belting and binding the earth? We reply all. It was the pressure of the weight of these strata as they fell to the earth, layer upon layer, fracturing and crushing into one another:

of a vast inland sea, covering more than half a million square miles; in the eyes of the geologists at least, we have one feature established that points to a deposit of light, primitive carbon from above, viz.: the fact that a *sea existed*, which was necessary for its distribution and deposition." *Story of the Rocks*, p.p. 162, 163.

three-fourths of our bodies, not less than four-fifths of every plant, and at least one-half of the solid rocks. More than twenty tons of pressure to the square inch is required to reduce oxygen to a liquid condition. This will give some idea of the chemical force by which it is held imprisoned in its liquid and solid forms. In a tumbler of water there are no less than six cubic feet of oxygen gas, condensed to a liquid state and held there by the continuous action of a force which can be measured only by hundreds of tons of pressure. Who can estimate the silent chemical power by which this subtle material is fitted for building the solid and abiding foundations of the earth?" *Natural Theology; or Rational Theism, by Prof. M. Valentine, D. D., LL. D., p.* 142.

1. The following words by Prof. Huxley, delivered in his New York lecture some years ago, sound as though he was an advocate of the *Bible chronology!!* He said: "It is perfectly certain that at a comparatively *recent* period of the world's history, that epoch which is written on the chart as the Cretaceous epoch it is perfectly certain that at that time, none of

the increasing pressure of the weight of strata upon strata, that first generated heat and finally fire which melted and fused the strata around it. Thus did the conglomerates and metals of our earth originate—by the pressure of the deposits one upon the other. (1) The fire which afterwards con-vulsed the earth and upheaved the "dry land." And the crushed and pulverized remains of the fractured and up-heaved strata furnishing the soil in which "grass, herbs and trees" were to germinate and grow, and afterwards again to be entombed.

To illustrate this feature of continent-making and mountain-range building more fully we will quote from an able thinker and geologist, who writes: "The great Mediterranean is certainly a grand example of the conservation,

---

the great physical features which at present mark the surface of the globe existed. It is certain that the Rocky Mountains were not. It is certain that the Himalaya Mountains were not. It is certain that the Alps and Pyrenes had not existence. The evidence of the simplest possible character, is simply this: We find raised up on the crags of these mountains, elevated by the forces of upheaval which have given rise to them, masses of cretaceous rock which formed the bottom of the sea before those mountains existed."

---

1. "Geologists until recently have spoken of granite as a primitive rock, as the nucleus of the earth, and as having been from time to time erupted, playing an important part in the general disturbances by which the framework of the earth is supposed to have been constructed. The observations of Daubree and Sorby show that all true granite had been elaborated with water, *under great pressure*, at a temperature below melting heat; that it had neither been ejected nor had it formed a framework. There are granites of all ages and of many kinds. Numerous observations show that granite alternates with, and passes into, stratified rocks, and must itself in such cases be stratified rock; and that its production does not necessarily involve the destruction and obliteration of all the stratified rocks with which it is associated. This view of the nature of granite will greatly affect the theories of geology."—*The Conversion of Stratified Rock into Granite, by Prof. Ansted, Read before the British Association, 1867.*

and transfer of energy. Many large rivers pour into it from all sides, bearing such enormous volumes of sediment, that is *not carried to the ocean*, but is constantly settling upon its bottom; and the frequent and appalling eruptions so well known in modern times, cannot but be pure results thereof. Can scientists find any other vents than volcanoes, and earthquakal agitations for this force employed? It must be accounted for. It cannot be lost. And the question might well be asked: Can volcanic eruptions have any other cause than that of transmitted or transferred energy? As we look around the globe to see all its volcanoes located in regions where transported sediment is accumulating, i. e. in, and around the ocean borders, and see that no volcanoes are located where no sediment can accumulate, can we for one moment doubt that we have here the true cause of volcanic eruptions. As the underlying rocks expand by the increase of heat, arising from additional sediment continually gathering upon them in the seas, they must fracture and crush into neighboring rocks; which crushing, must give rise to centres of fire susceptible of fusing the beds around them. And it is conceivable that sufficient sediment may gather over a bed of rock, to liquify the latter. About 65,000 feet of steel blocks, piled one upon another, will give rise to sufficient heat to melt the lowest blocks, or at least to render them plastic. Hence the reasonable conclusion, that the lava that issues from a volcano, is the deep bed rock fused by pressure, produced by lateral expansion. Thus we may behold even here the grand effort of solar action. Solar heat raises the vapor on high; it falls as rain, on hill and plain, swells into a stream, or feeds a fountain, and gathers sediment as it runs through its channels to the sea, where it adds its increment of mechanical heat to fuse the rock. So that the force employed in the grandest volcanic eruption, is the same in amount as that employed by the sunbeam, in raising that vapor from the sea to the clouds." (1)

Thus did all the metals and conglomerates originate (2) upon this our earth when "the waters which were *under* the firmament" were divided "from the waters which were *above* the firmament." The "measures thereof" having been established in "the beginning," the number thereof when the "light" began pouring its rays upon its own and the earth's canopy, and the binding up thereof when the

---

1. *The Story of the Rock*, by I. N. Vail, pp. 140, 141.

2. "Geology has been a revelation to mankind and has told us wonderful things of the past history of the earth. But geology has secrets of its own that are as hidden from comprehension as the atmosphere of the moon or the belts of Saturn. Certain things have been done, says the geologist, through volcanic action or the agency of fire, and that is as near as he can come to it. So that, after all, we see effects, but know little or nothing of causes. There is a rock known as amygadaloid, one of the igneous rocks, which in some of the gigantic transformations of nature, we will say in cooling from a melted state, formed within itself cavities from the size of a marble or bead to that of the closed hand. Now, as nature abhors a vacuum, she set to work to fill these cavities, and in doing so she used other materials, and these combinations produced some of what we call the 'precious stones of commerce.' Exactly how this was done we cannot tell, but we see some hint of the operation in every subterranean cave where stalactites and stalagmites are found. Every student knows that this is the result of dropping water which contains carbonate of lime. The water evaporating leaves a minute particle of lime, which takes something to itself from the earth or atmosphere, and in the course of time bodies are formed of a most remarkable character. In probably somewhat the same fashion have these cavities been filled in the igneous rocks, and then come time and storms and other agencies—earthquakes, perhaps—and the rocks are rent apart, and out drops a bead or a boulder, and a curious man picks it up, and hammers and breaks it, and then he puts a polish on it by some

"bars" and "doors" were "fastened" (1)—the expansion comprised between the water-level and that of the clouds—called "Heaven." For "that the work of this day was one performed on the clouds, would appear from Prov. 8: 27-29. the allusion of which to Gen. 1. is evident: 'When He established the heaven, I was there; when He set a circle upon the face of the deep; *when He made firm the skies above*; when the fountains of the deep became strong; when He gave to the sea its bound, the waters should not transgress his command; when He marked out the foundations of the earth.' " (2)

---

process more or less advanced, and lo! he holds in hi: :and an agate or an onyx.

"Many of the stones used in the arts have no other origin, and are deposits of silica, alumina, oxide of iron and other coloring substances. It is the color or the arrangement of colors that gives the name, and thus we have agate, onyx, chalcedony, carnelian, sard, chrysoprase, sardonyx and others, all members of the quartz family and all having a family resemblance. The agate has veins of different shades of color in parallel lines. Sometimes those are very close together, as many as fifty to the inch, but this is unusual. When there are alternate bands of color and a transparent medium we have the onyx; but the latter may be obtained by cutting the stone in a different way.   *   *   Nature produces some very strange forms occasionally, and agates are found with exact resemblances of moss and other natural objects and figures, which are very curious and often very valuable."—*American Analyst*, 1890.

---

1.   *Job* 38:4—11; *Job* 26:8—10.

2.   *Gennesis and Geology, by D. Crofton, p. 68.*

CHAPTER VI.

SEAS, CONTINENTS AND VEGETATION.

GEN. 1 : 9, 10, 11, 12, 13.

"And God said" in the morning of the third day, *"Let the waters under the heaven"*—expanse *"be gathered together unto one place,"* (1) subside in the moulds and depressed portions of the earth's surface, *"And let the dry land"*—those portions of the earth's crust designed for the future continents *"appear"* (Heb. RAAH—to be seen) *"and it was so."* *"And God called the dry land"* which appeared *"earth; and the gathering together of the waters, called He seas: And God saw that it was good."* (2) *"And God"* again *"said, Let the"* upheaved and dry *"earth put forth"* (Heb. DASHA—cause to germinate) *"grass, herb*

---

1. "The expression *'under the heaven,'* is evidently used to denote universality, *in universo terrarum orbe*; as in Job. 37:3. Compared, especially, Job. 28:24,—'He seeth under the whole heaven.' 'Let the waters be gathered together.'"—*The Six Days of Creation, by Prof. T. Lewis, p.* 123.

2. "The whole aspect of these passages. (Ps. 90:2; 104:6) taken in connection with the brief account in Genesis, gives strongly the impression that the place for the *gathering* and abiding of the waters was made by this upheaving action in the earth, the very action, if we say nothing now of duration, to which the geologist ascribes the growth and form of islands and continents."—*Six Days of Creation, by T. Lewis, p.* 127.

yielding seed, and fruit tree bearing fruit after its kind" (Heb. MIN—species) *"wherein is the seed thereof"*—that have seed in themselves: viz., have a power in their root, branch, leaves, buds or fruit, to propagate their species, *"upon the earth: and it was so."* (1) *"And the earth brought forth"* (Heb. YATSA—cause to go out) *"grass,"*—in the sediment of the ruptured and upheaved strata; for the ascending seething vapors from the waters of the *"seas"* just lodged in their beds of hot and burning strata, produced a climate mild and warm for it to germinate.

---

1. "The origination of organic Life in Nature remains an open question. Our knowledge extends at present only to its reproduction and increase. To these there is a sufficient key in well known laws; and they may be carried to any extent without demanding the supposition of other than familiar agencies and established principles. But the question of the first arising of the living state, the primary direction of the chemical or other force to produce an organic arrangement of the elements, remain as yet undecided. There is no difficulty in conceiving such a modification of chemical action to arise in accordance with the natural laws, and that there should be forces existing which must operate, under given circumstances, to determine the organic arrangement of elements when it does not exist before. Indeed, M. Berthelot's magnificent experiments, in which some of the simpler organic substances have been formed from their elements by the application of force in the laboratory, seem to exhibit this very fact before our eyes. And the differences pointed out by Professor Graham between the two great divisions of matter (the crystalling, and the colloidal or gelatinous) have a most suggestive bearing in the same direction. He remarks respecting the latter (or colloidal) substances, that they contain force; 'the probable primary source of the force appearing in the phenomena of vitality.' He shows, too, that there are many other forms of this kind of matter besides the organic: the hydrated silicic acid, for example, from which in geologic periods flint appears to have been formed. He compares these substances to water kept from freezing at a temperature below 32 deg., or to a saline solution more than saturated with the salt, and ready to crystallize on the slightest shock: —a condition of tension

"*Herb yielding seed after its kind, and tree bearing fruit, wherein is the seed thereof after its kind,*" a permanent feature and characteristic of trees. "*God saw that it*" the work of this day "*was good;*" in the clouds, upon the surface of the earth, and in the varieties of seeds;—all together allwise in their arrangements, perfect in their execution, and well fitted for their respective ends. "*And there was evening,*" the darkness which closed the second day, "*and there was morning,*" the light which introduced the next day "*a third day.*"

The thoughtful reader has, doubtless, observed that the only instance when the work of creation was not pronounced "*good,*" occurred at the close of the second day. The plain reason for this omission was, that the work was

---

essentially the same as that which is the great distinction of the organic substances. But still we do not know in what way the organic state of matter may have arisen in nature. We are equally in the dark, indeed, as to the origination of any of the other forces or arrangements of the elements; and the entire body of our knowledge must be advanced before we can satisfactorily discuss it. The difficulty is increased by the absolutely contradictory results, hitherto, of the experiments made by different observers to ascertain whether organized bodies arise in infusions of vegetable matter, without the presence of germs from which they may be developed. Each man will probably entertain his own opinion. My own is, that both organic matter and organized creatures did probably, and possibly may still, arise in the ordinary course of nature. And I am confirmed in this opinion by the emphatic language (three times repeated) of Genesis: 'And God said, let the earth bring forth grass, the herb yielding seed, and the fruit tree yielding fruit after his kind, whose seed is in itself upon the earth: and it was so. And the earth brought forth grass, and herb yielding seed after his kind, and the tree yielding fruit, whose seed was in itself after his kind.' Gen. 1: 11, 12.' And again: 'And God said, let the waters bring

not yet completed,—the process of division in the atmosphere, the separation of the sea and dry land, and the creation of grass, herbs and trees,—had not yet been
effected.   (1)

The Psalmist, besides eulogizing the power and majesty
of the Creator in the most forcible language when he says:
"O Lord my God, thou art very great; Thou art clothed
with honor and majesty. Who coverest Thyself with light
as with a garment; Who stretchest out the heavens like a
curtain; Who layeth the beams of His chambers in the
waters;   *   *   His ministers flaming fire." Also particularly emphasizes the *modus operandi* of the work of the
third day. He writes: "Who laid the foundations" (Heb.
YASAD—founded the earth upon her basis) "of the earth,

---

forth abundantly the moving creature that hath life, and fowl that may fly
above the earth in the open firmament of heaven. And God created great
whales and every living creature that moveth, which the waters brought
forth abundantly after their kind.' Gen. 1; 20, 21. And again: 'And God
said, let the earth bring forth the living creature after his kind, cattle and
creeping things and beasts of the earth after his kind; and it was so.'
Gen. 1: 24.

"It is indeed remarkable that in the teeth of these words the religious
sentiments of men should have been roused against the opinion that the
earth and the waters brought forth, or might be supposed probably to have
brought forth, living creatures.   *   *   *   We dismiss, however, as

---

1. "M. Barrandi, after noticing the fact that no trilobites are found
below the Silarian rocks, though remains of plants and marine worms are
preserved there, and that the trilobites appear at once in great abundance,
thus comments upon its bearing upon Darwinianism: 'All these sudden
manifestations of life under new typical forms, appearing constantly and
everywhere with the plenitude of their distinctive characters, are in complete discord with the hypothesis of a gradual development by insensible
and successive variations, since such a transformation can only be wrought
out through an indefinite series of intermediate forms, of which no trace
has been found in any country.' "— *Errors of Evolution*, p. 231.

that it should not be moved forever. Thou coverest it with
the deep" (Heb. THEHOM of Gen. 1:2,) "as with a vesture:
The waters stood above the mountains. At Thy rebuke they
fled; * * They went up by the mountains, They
went down by the valleys." (Literal, the mountains rose,
the valleys sank down,). Unto the place which Thou hast
founded for them. Thou hast set a bound" (Heb. GEBUL—
an enclosed place) "that they may not pass over; (1) That
they turn" (Heb. SHUB—to turn back) "not again to cover
the earth. He sendeth forth springs into the valleys; They
run among the mountains; They give drink to every beast
of the field; * * By these the fowl of the heaven
have their habitation, they sing" (Literal, utter their voices)
"among the branches. * * The earth is satisfied

---

premature, any discussion of the origin of organic life, or consequently of
the vital force. But we perceive that from our present point of view the
vital force exists simply in a peculiar arrangement of elements, involving
a tension of a special kind. By whatsoever means this arrangement may
be produced, the force thus embodied in it is equally called vital. The
characters of the force are due to that arrangement; they flow from it
rather than are concerned in its production; just as in the case of the other
forces, such as heat or electricity, the peculiar properties they manifest are
the results and not the causes of the states of matter in which they consist. * * The vital force, then, is like the other forces in nature in
this, that it causes, or exists in, a state of tension; it is peculiar in respect
to the characters of the tension in which it is exhibited. One of these characters is so striking and universal as to deserve especial mention. An almost constant process in the rendering inorganic matter organic is the
giving off of oxygen; as constant, in the return to the inorganic state, is its
absorption. The whole process may be said to constitute a great de-oxidation and re-oxidation; the de-oxidation produced by force and constituting

---

1. Prof. Dana rightfully claims that the foundation—outlines and
boundaries of the continents are of old.—*The Author.*

with the fruit of Thy works.   He causeth the grass to grow
for cattle, and herb for the service of man;   *   *
And wine that maketh glad the heart of man."   (1)

But let us also hear science explain how the "dry land"
was to appear and "the gathering together of the waters"
was to become seas.   The "more than 40,000 feet of Archæan
beds   *   *   formed as sediments from the first ocean,
it was *that* much of the mineral and metallic frame, each
a foot of thickness only adding weakness to the mighty
casement of the earth.   The lowest beds possessed a certain
degree of heat as a result of mechanical pressure, and possessed certain dimensions resulting from that degree of heat.
The waters at that time had their beds; and as those beds
deepened, the mechanical pressure in such places increased
on account of the gravitation of waters thither.   This increase of pressure augmented the heat of the lower beds;
this augmentation increased their dimensions and necessarily
produced local plication.   This occurring in the deep seated

---

a tension, the re-oxidation a return, a rebound as it were, to the former
state, reproducing the force.   And on the constant supply of oxygen all
functional power, and therewith the continuance of the life, depends.   The
living body and the atmosphere around it constitute an inseparable whole.
The once united elements still retain, in reality, their coherence— put asun-
der by force, and for temporary purposes, but pledged as it were to a deeper
and inviolable union.   In the re-uniting of the parted elements is effected
the end and object of the whole process, the functions of animal life.
Complex, wonderful and beautiful as it is, surely the wonder and beauty
of the organic world rise in this view to a yet greater height.   For in the
de-oxidation and re-oxidation of the hydrogen in a single drop of water, we
have before us, truly, so far as force is concerned, an epitome of the whole
life."—*Life in Nature, by James Hinton, pp. 15, 16, H. Ed.*

---

1.   *Ps.* 104:1—15.

beds, naturally forced rocks between others, and this from necessity produced elevation upon the surface. Here the evolution of continents began. But this beginning was not until late in the Archæan times. This continent-making and strata-bending did not take place until the Laurentian period closed. For the conglomerates and coarser and beds which show violent agitation and movement of waters, lie uncomformably upon the lower beds." (1)

"The scene which the surface of our planet at this eventful hour presented, must have been one of supreme and terrific grandeur. * The land, as elevated from the depths * * was, of course, bare and barren, the hollowed valleys, the oozy plains, and the trickling mountain sides, were alike destitute of all vegetation; no tree, no bushes, no grass, as yet, adorned the wet and slimy ground. But this condition of things was to be of short duration." On the self same day, when the climate became mild and warm, through the ascending seething vapors from the waters of the "seas" just lodged in their beds of depressed and upheaved, hot and burning strata; and this, after the sediments of the ruptured strata were deposited among the boulders and pebbles of the previous eruptions of the earth's surface, to furnish the soil and environment for the coming vegetation; then "the word went forth that stocked the earth with all sorts of trees, and shrubs, and herbs, and grasses, which were endowed with power to reproduce and spread their kind till the earth was

---

1. *Story of the Rocks*, p. 218. *Dana's Manual*, p. 150.

covered, and to perpetuate their respective species to the end of time." (1)

What a lofty demonstration of the wisdom and goodness of God do we here discover, even in the very midst of these vast and fearful convulsions of the earth's crust, and in the "grass, herb yielding seed, and fruit tree bearing fruit after its kind" which were to germinate and grow upon the upheaved continents. (2) Were they not the prophetic forms of what was to follow—were not these "earlier organic forms to forshadow and predict others that were to succeed them in time?" Thus "a principal of adaptation to special ends prevades all existence, and that it must be assumed as the ground of scientific explanation of the facts and phenomena of the universe, is avowed by the first scientists of the age. 'We can not be content,' says Dr. Laycock, 'with simply determining the mere relation of things or events— an existence, a co-existence, a succession, or a resemblance —and not inquire into the *ends* thereof. Such a doctrine

---

1. *The Terrible Catastrophe or Biblical Deluge. Illustrated and corroborated by Tradition, Mythology and Geology. To which is added a Brief Interpretation of Creation, by Rev. G. C. H. Hasskarl, pp. 264, 265.*

2. "The globe, notwithstanding all the changes through which it has passed, has not been diminished or increased in size or bulk. The indestructibility of matter is an axiom in physics. And I may add, that, an atom of matter is just as uncreatable as it is indestructible—that is to say, a new particle of matter can no more be brought into existence, than an atom already in existence can be destroyed, without the power of Him Who created it at the first. Therefore, this globe retains the size and weight imparted to it in the morn of creation. It has lost nothing -it has gained nothing. There are certain changes going on. Old affinities may be broken op, but new ones will be formed. Every element, and even every atom has its special mission, and their missions they will perform. The particle of moisture that glistens, in the early morn, as a dewdrop on some beautiful

applied to physiology would, in fact, arrest all scientific research into the phenomena of life; for the investigation of the so-called functions of organs is nothing more than a *teleological* investigation.' '*A law of design is the higher generalization of the great uniformities of nature.*' In his inaugural address at the meeting of the British Association of Science at Edinburg, Sir Wm. Thomson said: 'I feel profoundly convinced that the argument from design has been greatly lost sight of in recent speculations. * * Overwhelmingly strong proofs of intelligence and benevolent design lie all around us; and if even perplexities, whether of a metaphysical or scientific character, turn us away for a time, they will come back upon us with irresistible force, showing us through nature the influence of a *Free Will*, and teaching us that all living beings depend upon one ever-acting *Creator and Ruler.*'

"Every enlargement of our knowledge of organic nature is an addition to the already numberless instances of recognized special adaptation which crowd us on every hand;

---

flower, may once have trembled as a tear in some weeping eye, or sparkled in the sunlight on the crest of an ocean wave, or been crystallized into a beautiful snow-flake lighting down on some alpine summit, or, it may be, passed into the life-current that has beat at some breaking heart. I say that all the elements are obedient to the will of God, and to the mission which He has assigned them in the economy of the universe There is a constant equilibrium maintained. You see the ocean is always sending up its watery vapors. But the ocean is always full. The vapors go up in clouds, and descend in rain, and are poured into the ocean again. It is just so with the atmosphere. It goes from the south to the north, and from the north to the south, but it is never exhausted. Not a particle is ever wasted. It circulates and circulates, and heaves the lungs of man and beast the world over, but it never tires of its mission, and not a particle is ever wasted, etc."—*Moses and the Philosophers, by S. A. Hodgman, M. J. C.,* pp. 89, 90.

and all scientific discovery is but an illustration and a veri-
fication of the *apriori* intuition of the reason that a principle
of design is co-extensive with the the highest law of the
universe.   Not merely of each individual existence, but of
the grand totality of existence, are we constrained to believe
that it exists for a purpose.   Above all special ends there is
a great ultimate design of creation—a last and final end to
which all intermediate ends are means: and though physical
science can not fully compass that final purpose, yet in the
light of its present knowledge of special ends it has abundant
reason for assuming that there *must* be a final purpose, and
that that final purpose is at once beneficent and wise."   (1)

1.   *Theistic Conception of the World, pp.* 129, 130.

CHAPTER VII.

THE LIGHT-BEARERS.

GEN. 1 : 14, 15, 16, 17, 18, 19.

"*And God said*" in the dawn of the fourth day, "*let there be lights*" (Heb. MEAROTH—light-bearers) (1) —illuminators "*in the firmament of the heaven*" which are "*to divide the day from the night*"—to divide between the day and between the night; "*and let them be for signs*" to all the living, signs of the power, wisdom and goodness of God, "*and for seasons*" (2)—by their steady progression in their orbits they would bring *eventually* the different seasons in their rotation, "*and for days*" to measure out the alternation of day and night, "*and years*"—the grand division of time by

---

1. "The Hebrew word employed in verse 14 (MEAROTH) which is unfortunately rendered 'lights' in the Authorized (and Revised) Version, is a different word from the 'light' (OR) of verse 3-5. MEAROTH strictly means 'light-bearers,' or bodies giving light. This distinction is carefully observed in the LXX., DeWette, Benisch, Kalish, Tuch, Knobel, Delitzsch, and Keil. The fourth creative formation was the establishment of such cosmical conditions or relations as should enable the heavenly bodies to fulfill their light-giving functions to the earth."—*Dr. Cocker's Theistic Conception of the World, p.* 154.

2. "Gesenius interprets for 'signs, and for seasons' by *en dia dnoin* as if it were, for 'signs of seasons,' "—*Genesis and Geology, p.* 69.

which all successions of duration are distinguished, and
which they would also continue to describe and determine without cessation or mistake : *"and let them"*—
these appointed illuminators *"be for lights"* (Heb.
LIEROTH) *"in the firmament of heaven to give light
upon the earth: and it was so."* (1) *"And God
made"*—ordained them—*"the two great lights"* (Heb.
HAMEOROTH—the light-bearers) *"the greater light"*
—the sun, the elements of which were not here first
created—*"to rule the day; and the lesser light"*—the
moon, the substance of which existing from the beginning with the earth—*"to rule the night:"* *"He made
the stars also"* to appear in the firmament of the heaven.
"And God set"—placed *"them in the firmament of the*

───────────────────

1. "All modern science compels us to posit as starting point a primo-
dial state of the universe in which its various masses, molecules, and atoms
stood apart, from one another at unknown distances. But each particle had
inherent in it those forces which were destined in the future to effect its
aggregation with every other.

"The universe as a whole has a common centre of gravity, towards
which all its various masses are attracted. Those masses still possess potential energy in virtue of their separation from one another and from this
central point of union; and it is clear that if they were to aggregate sud-
denly around that point, their potential energy would become kinetic as
they fell, and would be transmuted into heat as they clashed together at the
common cosmical meeting-place. It would then be radiated off into the
ether, and the matter would gradually assume a solid and perfectly aggregated form. Now, it is possible that some of the sideral masses may be thus
gravitating towards the common centre in a direct line; and if they are
then it is clear that their motion is the correlative of their previous separation. But it is more probable that the various suns are prevented from aggregating directly with one another by some form of continuous motion.
We are sure in the case of the best-known large masses—the earth and other

heaven to give light upon the earth;" (1) and thus by the diffusion of light *"to rule over the day and over the night, and to divide the light from the darkness: and God saw that it was good. And there was evening"*— the darkness that closed the third day *"and there was morning"*—the light that followed *"a fourth day."*

In the works of the previous day our attention was directed to the great problems of the geology of our planet; how that the dry land appeared, the waters retired to their ocean beds, and the earth was invested with all the variety and beauty of grasses, herbs, and fruit-bearing trees. And who can tell what additional layers of strata found in the

---

planets—that they are prevented from aggregating with their relative centre, the sun, by the continuous energy of their orbital motion. We also know that certain special suns—the double stars—have such a relative motion with regard to one another. We further know that all stars have a proper motion whose cycle is so immense that it cannot be measured by the short period of human observation. It is probable, therefore, that the ascertained cause which prevents central aggregation in the known cases (namely, orbital motion) may be fairly extended to the unknown cases. We may conclude, accordingly, that all the heavenly bodies are prevented from aggregating around the common cosmical centre of gravity owing to their possession of a relative orbital movement. Of course, there may be many cycles of such orbital movements one within the other, as we know to be the case with the satellites which circle round a planet, while the planet circles round the sun, and the sun has his own proper motion. All that is contended here is merely this—that each mass or set of masses is probably prevented from aggregating with each other mass or set of masses, around their relative centre, or around the absolute cosmical centre, by some continuous kinetic energy, analogous to the known orbital motion of the planets and their satellites."—*Force and Energy, etc., by G. Allen, p. 32.*

---

1. *Jer.* 31:35; *Ps.* 104:18.

Silurian beds, and in the calcareous and carbonaceous matter of the Devonean formation, descended from the "curtain"
(1) of "waters" (1) which canopied and belted the earth, and
in which the "grass, herbs and fruit-bearing trees" after
germination, here again partially entombed, to lay dormant
for a season and afterwards to re-invest the continents and
islands with their variety and beauty? (2) For the Astro-
logical changes of this fourth day,—the "Age of Rain" as
science has been pleased to call it, when the sun and the
other planets of our system were for the first time to rotate
together as they do to-day—certainly very materially
affected and disturbed the aqueous matter-rings of the higher
atmosphere of the earth. Before the light of the "lights"—
light-bearers and illuminators—could at all penetrate the
seething streams of the firmament of the heavens, change
the dark and cloudy horizon of the earth's first morning
from bronze into golden hues, who knows, what these adjustments and collocations were; what downfalls occurred,
and how the vegetation and the inhabitants of the seas were
affected? For even in this period of the earth's history the

---

1. *Ps.* 104: 2, 3.

2. That forms of life still exist which have come down through all the
changes from very early periods, is evident from the *Lingulae and the
Nautili*, which have survived even from the Cambria period until now.
Again, that plants and animals according to the record of creation have a
common origin, is also confirmed by science; for says *Prof. G. L. Goodale*,
in his address before The American Association for the Advancement of
Science, in 1889, on "Some Recent Investigations Relative to Cell-contents,"
after an able review of the origin of the term and the use of the word
"*protoplasm*;" that "all the work in the contiguous fields of botany and
zoology has made no physical or chemical distinction between the living
matter in animals and plants."—*Proceedings of the American Association for
the Advancement of Science.* p. 265, 1889.

"greater and lesser" lights, no more than garnished the heavens with their diffused rays; and these original "lights" were in after centuries to adjust the day and the night, the seasons and the years? An upper sea of great waves, separated from the transparent firmament, still concealed and hid the "lights" from the earth.

If Moses had stated, that the sun and moon had appeared, not on the first, but on the *fourth* day, he certainly would have blundered. But observe, with what accuracy Moses makes his statements, how widely he separates the development of the earth from the development of the sun's light. "It required a much longer time for these changes to pass upon the sun than upon the earth, for the sun is more than 1,200,000 times larger than the earth; and the time required to work important changes bears some proportion to the bulk." (1) How then were the "grass, herbs, and fruit-bearing trees" to germinate and grow? We reply, simply by the temperature and climate which were transmitted to the earth's surface by the light and heat, which penetrated through the sun's and the earth's canopy of vapors; together with the heat of the warm vapors arising to the firmament above, from the waters of the "seas" coming in contact with the hot and burning strata just upheaved. The sun therefore was not known to the early human race otherwise than *a lighter;* and first only after the darkness of the sun's canopy had been dispersed and dissipated, and the outermost aqueous-rings of the mundane firmament had fallen to the

---

1. *Dr. Chapin.*

earth; then it (the sun) was known as *a lighter* and *a heater.*
(1)   Here the language of Scripture, on whose pages no contradictions are found, again becomes our witness; for the word from which the term "lights" is derived in the Hebrew, is in no possible sense synonymous with the words which mean sun or moon, and which in fact, the reader will find used first after the Deluge, when men in truth could see and feel the presence of these lights.

Then first did these "lights" become "signs to all the living,—signs of the power, wisdom and goodness of God,—signs to the mariner of his course on the trackless deep,—signs to the husbandman for sowing his seed and gathering his harvest,—signs to the traveller in tracing his path through the gloom of the forest, or over the wilds of the desert; "and for seasons,"— by their steady progression in their appointed orbits they would bring on spring and summer, autumn and winter in their due rotation; "and for days," by their established revolutions they would measure out the alternation of day and night, "and years"—the grand

---

1. "Nothing is more remarkable, even to the present state of physical science, than the fact that, under the subtile analysis of modern physics, much that we have been accustomed to regard as phenomena of matter dissolves and disappears, surviving only as phenomena of *Force.* The phenomena of heat, light, color, sound, electricity, and magnetism are now 'modes of motion'—manifestations of one and the same omnipresent energy, which is transferred from one portion of matter to another, and modified or transformed simply by the mechanical arrangements and collocations of matter. The opinion is rapidly gaining ground that even chemical action is a mode of motion, and Professor Norton does not hesitate in affirming that '*all the phenomena of material nature result from the action of force upon matter.*' All that we mean by a Material Force 'is a force which acts upon matter, and produces in matter its own appropriate effects.' It is not an attribute of matter, not a quality inherent in matter, but a mode or state superimposed upon matter." *Theistic Conception of the World, pp.* 122, 123.

division of time by which all succession of duration is distinguished, and which they would also continue to describe and determine without cessation or mistake.   (1)   Thus did God make provisions on this fourth day of creation, sixteen hundred years before and ever since man has been enabled to behold the sun and moon in the earth's firmament ceaselessly and efficiently performing their mission.   .

An able author expresses himself in the following manner on the works of this day.   He writes: "I must now remark upon two passages of Gen. 2, which appear to confirm the view that assigns the first creation of all things to 'the beginning' and the preparation of our earth to the 'six days.' The first of these is in verse 3, 'God blessed the seventh day, and sanctified it; because that in it He had rested from all His work which God created and made' (Literal, 'God created to make').   The 'creation' and 'making' are not identified as an act; they are rather individualized, and distinguished from each other, and the former placed antecedently to the latter, a position well according with a 'creation' in 'the beginning,' and subsequent 'making' on the 'six days.'

"The second phrase is in verse 4: 'These *are* the generations of the heavens and of the earth when they were created' (BEHIBAREAM) 'in the day the Lord God made' (ASOTH) 'the earth and the heavens.' This also seems to distinguish between the 'creation' and 'making,' and to show

---

1.   *The Terrible Catastrophe, &c.,* pp. 272, 273.

that the account in Gen. 1. refers principally to 'days.' (1)
This appears from continuation of the passage, verse 5: 'and
every plant of the field before it was in the earth, and every
herb of the field before it grew:' evidently alluding to chapter 1: 11.   I think it worth remarking, that we here find
reason also to expect so much of our planets history as was
absolutely necessary, or, if not so. why the particularization
'in the day, that the Lord God made the earth and the
heavens.'   Why not a detail of everything concerning the
earth, consecutively to 'These *are* the generations of the
heavens and of the earth when they were created.' "   (2)

1.   Unfortunately the writer here separates the *first* verse of Genesis
from the verses that follow.   But this does not in the least invalidate his
excellent scriptural argument.   *The Author.*

2.   *Genesis and Geology, by Denis Crofton, p. 91-93.*

CHAPTER VIII

SEA-MONSTERS AND BIRDS.

GEN. 1 : 20, 21, 22, 23.

"*And God said, let the waters*" of the "seas" be the element and place to "*bring forth abundantly*" (Lit. —Swarm with swarms of living creatures,) "*the moving*"—ra, idly multiplying "*creature that hath life, and let fowl*"—all the living creatures that can raise themselves into the air by means of wings, insects, as well as birds; "*fly above the earth in the open firmament of heaven*" (Lit.—That may fly on the face of the expanse of the heaven,). "*And God created*" (Heb. BARA) "*the great sea-monsters, and every living creature that moveth*" (Literal—that hath a soul of life,) (1)—reptiles and amphibious animals, "*which the waters brought*

---

1. Life itself, like many other things, eludes all definition. We only know that it is an organizing principle or power, of which there are three forms differing in manifestation. These forms are vegetable life, known by growth; animal life, known by locomotion; and spiritual life, known by rationality, consciousness and moral feeling. *The Author.*

"It is through *life*, that organism lives and moves and has its being, but *the life itself* we cannot see. We cannot weigh it in balances. We cannot measure its form or dimensions. We cannot touch its body or substance. We cannot hear the sound of its coming or going;—it is invisible, indivisible, and inconceivable.

"The person who attempts to *explain* life, be it that of the plant or the brute, the animal, temporal life of man, called in the New Testament *psuche,*

forth abundantly" by the command of God *"after their kinds and every winged fowl after its kind: and God saw that it was good."*   *"And God blessed them,"* that is, God gave them power to propagate their species by generation, to increase into a countless multitude, *"saying, be fruitful and multiply. and fill the waters in the seas, and let the fowl multiply in the earth. And there was evening"*—the darkness of the previous day *"and there was morning"*—the light which followed *"a fifth day."*   (1)

"It is remarkable that both the record of nature and the record of the Bible concur in ascribing the origin and

---

or the religious life, both as enjoyed here and as continued hereafter, called in the New Testament *zoe*; even the varied manifestations of it, in the inorganic or organic, the terrestrial or celestial; might as well attempt to define Eternity, describe the God of all creation, the Author of all life, as He exists in the far back depths of that Eternity." – *The Author in his Work on Evolution as Taught in the Bible, p. 27.*

"All the force, all the heat, all the motion, in the non-living universe is incompetent to develop a living monad; and this the physicists know." *Protoplasm, or Matter of Life, by Lionel Beale, p. 250.*

"A mechanical origin of the first organisms from inorganic matter, has thus been proved,   *   *   to be a necessary hypothesis." – *History of Creation, by Dr. Haeckel, Vol. 2, p. 278.*

"Whence is life? Creation by law, evolution by law, development by law, or, as including all those kindred ideas, the reign of law, is nothing but the reign of creative force directed by creative knowledge, worked under the control of creative power, and in fulfilment of creative purpose." *Reign of Law, by Duke of Argyll, p. 253. Quoted in Evolution as Taught in the Bible, p. 40.*

---

1. "The unity of plan in beings so diverse as, a fish, a bird, a man, is conclusive proof of their creation of one intelligent Creator." – *Robert Patterson.*

earliest existence of animal life (1) to the sea, where we are
told there are 'creeping things innumerable.' The sea is
even yet the great storehouse of animal life, and it would
seem   *   *   *   to have been the only theatre of
its development. This great cosmical truth, revealed to the
ancient Hebrew prophet, is not without its scientific significance. In a *physiological* point of view, it indicates the important fact that the conditions of animal life are easier in
the sea than on the land. There both the most minute and
the grandest forms of life can find suitable conditions, and
there the feebler tissues and the less energetic vitality can
succeed in the battle of life. In the *geological* relations, it
shows that it was necessary that the land itself, to be suitable to the support of the higher forms of life, must be born
from the sea, and that the action of marine organisms in

---

1. "The gist of our present inquiry regarding the introduction of life
is this: Does it belong to what we call matter? or was it inserted into
matter at some suitable epoch—say, when the physical condition became
such as to permit the development of life?" "However the convictions
here and there may be influenced, the process must be slow which commends the process of natural evolution to the public mind. For what are
the core and essence of this hypothesis? Strip it naked and you stand face
to face with the notion, that not alone the mere ignoble forms of the horse
and lion, not alone the exquisite wonderful mechanism of the human body,
but that the human mind itself—emotion, intellect, will, and all their phenomena—were once latent in a fiery cloud. Surely the mere statement is
more than a refutation." "I do not think that any holder of the evolution
hypothesis would say that I have misstated it in any way; I have merely
stripped it of all vagueness, and bring before you unclothed and unvar-
nished, the notions by which it must stand or fall. Surely these notions
represent an absurdity too monstrous to be entertained by any sane mind."
—*Prof. Tyndall in a paper read by him before the British Association, cited in
"Christianity and Positivism," p. 31.*
On this subject of evolution, *Prof. Dr. Franz Delitzsch,* of the Leipzig
University, Germany, expresses himself in the following manner in a letter
which the author received from him. Among other things he writes: "Die

heeping up beds of their skeletons was one of the necessary preparations for the actual condition of our continents. Both records give us a grand procession of dynasties of life, beginning from the lower forms and culminating in man." (1)

"All previous animals that we know had respired in the water by means of gills or similar apparatus. Now we have animals which must have been able to draw in the vital air into capacious chambered lungs, and with this power must have enjoyed a far higher and more active style of vitality; and must have possessed the faculty of uttering truly vocal sounds. What wondrous possibilities unknown to these creatures, perhaps only dimly perceived by such rational intelligence as may have watched the growth of our young world, were implied in these gifts! It is one of the remark-

---

verschiedenen Species der Creaturen bilden eine aufsteigende Scala, aber nich so dass eine Species sich aus der andern entwickelt. Die biblische Schœpfungs Idee ist durchaus anti-Darwinistisch, und sie wird durch die Erfahrung nicht widerlegt, sondern bestätigt. Evolution im biblischen Sinne, ist Entwucklung, der vom dem Schœpfer in die einzelnen Species der Creaturen gelegte Triebkraft Kein Microscop kann diese in den Protophasmen liegende unterschiedliche praiformation zu unterscheiden, diese praiformatire ist das Werk und Geheimniss des Schœpfer. Gott ist es der den Bestand der Welt schœpferisch begrundet hat und ihn erhält. Die Begrundung war ein Mirackel und die Erhaltung ist ein Mirackel. Vergeblichsucht die Wissenschaft den Gott, welcher alle in Wunder thut, zu Eliminiren." *Sir J. Wm. Dawson, L.L, D., of McGill University, Montreal, Canada,* expresses himself thus in a letter to the author: "I have ceased to write anything on evolution, except when it comes in the way in treating of other matter. * * It appears to me to lie outside of the domain of legitimate science, and to be a philosophical fancy which, like others that have preceded it, must run its course." *The Author.*

---

1. *Dr. Dawson quoted in The Terrible Catastrophe or Biblical Deluge, etc. by Rev. G. C. H. Hasskarl, p. 288-290.*

able points in the history of creation in Genesis, that this step of the creative work is emphatically marked. Of all creatures we have noticed up to this point, it is stated that God said, 'Let the waters bring forth;' but here it is said 'God *created* not, whales, but *reptiles*.'" (1)

"Birds are described as being brought into existence *after* fishes and sea monsters. This position of birds in the Mosaic record is remarkably in accordance with the geological chronology of their appearance. The earliest traces of birds yet discovered are in the Triassic period; and it is only in the chalk period, just after the reign of great sea monsters and reptiles of the Wealden, that birds appear to any extent in the fossil remains. (2) Birds are the most distinctive and best characterized class in the whole animal kingdom. There is a constancy in the nature of their covering which does not admit of the variations found in mammals, reptiles and fishes; for every bird brings forth its young alive, or produces them in no other way than from eggs, consisting invariably of yolk, white and calcareous shell, and

---

1. *Terrible Catastrophe or Biblical Deluge*, pp. 202, 203.

2. "The Lingula family is represented by species in our present seas; and so also the Discina and Nautilus families. Among Vertebrates some of ancient Gars are very much like our modern kinds, and on Triassic genus, *ceratodus*, is still represented in Australian seas. Such facts, coming up from the past, through ages of unceasing change, declare emphatically the unity of system in nature.

"This truth is further manifested, in the fact of a *general parallelism between the progress of the earth's life and the successive phases in embryonic development*. The almost egg-like simplicity of the earliest living species of the rocks—the Rhizopods among animals, the Infusorial plants,—is the first illustration Geology presents.

"The earliest Crustaceans of the Phyllopod group closely resemble the young of some of the higher groups of living Crustaceans; and the early

incubated by artificial heat. No bird deviates in its skeleton from the typical form, as the whale does among mammals, and the serpent among reptiles. No bird deviates from the ordinary mode of generation of its class, as do the marsupials from other quadrupeds." (1)

These are the new creations of this day:—the word itself, BARA (to create) being used here for the first time since the record in the first verse. What had been done and made in the interval between was the mere re-arrangement of existing matter; now first is life introduced, and it required not simply construction, but *creative* power. The three expressions "great sea monsters, every living creature that moveth, every winged fowl after its kind," are introduced so as to embrace all forms of life in the air and water. Life itself, like many other things, eludes all definition. We only know that it is an organizing principle or power, of which there are three forms, differing in manifestation. These forms are vegetable life, known by growth; animal life, known by locomotion; and spiritual life, known by

Fishes have cartilaginous skeletons, just as is now true of the higher Vertebrates when in the embryonic condition.

"Again, the Gars of the present day have a vertebrated lobe to the tail, which they lose on becoming adults; and so the Gars had vertebrated tails in the young world, which feature was lost in the progress of the Mesozoic era. The Amphiblans afford a very similar illustration. So also the birds; for, as the young often have a tail of several disconnected vertebrae, which contracts much on passing to the adult stage, so the earliest known of the bird type had long, vertebrated tails, such as no modern bird can boast and complain of."—*Manual of Geology, by James D. Dana, L.L. D., pp. 594, 595, 3d Edition.*

1. *Dr. Tristram, quoted in The Terrible Catastrophe, pp. 293, 294.*

rationality, consciousness and moral feeling. And it was in virtue of the first blessing here pronounced that the life animating the tribes of the air and sea have continued to multiply and increase to the present day.

Well has it been said: "The beginnings of the characteristic of an age are to be looked for in the midst of a preceding age; and marks of the future coming out to view are prophetic of that future. The age of mammals was foreshadowed by the appearance of mammals long before, in the course of Reptilian age. And the age of Reptiles was prophesied in types that lived in the earlier carboniferous age. Such is the system in all history." (1) "The life of all these geological periods is full of mute prophesies, to be read only in the light of subsequent fulfillment;" (2)—a conception not the less true of even the material changes which are set forth in the creative week itself. For observe only how that the dividing of "the waters *under* the firmament from the waters *above* the firmament" produced the most extraordinary changes in the earth's canopy and upon its surface; how that the placing of the "greater and lesser lights" in the firmament again very materially affected the aqueous matter-rings and the vaporized metals and minerals, causing them to fall in deposits—strata of a uniform thickness the world over; and how these very downfalls in deposits became the cause,—the pressure of the weight of these strata upon strata,—of the upheaval of "dry land"

---

1. *Manual of Geology, p.* 137.

2. *Story of the Earth and Man, by Sir J. Wm. Dawson, L.L. D., p.* 78, *8th Edition.*

and the depressions of the "seas," having produced earthquakes and volcanic eruptions by their weight. These changes or as science has expressed it "exterminations" (1) were in truth "remarkable for their universality;" for they produced all that bound and belted the earth, above it, around it, and upon it.

---

1. "It will be necessary to consider a difficulty which, to many minds, has presented itself, from the fact of the discoveries of geology having shown the existence of physical suffering and death amongst the brute creation, throughout ages ante-cedent to the introduction of sin into the world by our first parents. This appears to arise from a too hasty generalization of those passages which denounce death as the penalty of transgression, Gen. 2: 17; Rom. 5: 12; 6:23; James 1: 15, etc.; but upon examination nothing will be found in them to warrant anything further than the belief that sin brought death upon the *human* race. It will be necessary to consider Rom. 8: 20-22, a little more in detail. We here find, 'for the creature' (*ektisis*) 'was made subject to vanity, not willingly, but by reason of him who hath subjected *the same* in hope, because the creature itself also shall be delivered from the bondage of corruption into the glorious liberty of the children of God. For we know that the whole creation' (*pasa e ktisis*) 'groaneth and travaileth in pain together until now. It is evident that the inference to be drawn from this passage depends upon the interpretation given to the phrases *e ktisis* and *pasa e ktisis*, whether they be applied to the whole creation, or only to the human species. That the latter signification is to be considered the correct one appears from the only places in the New Testament where *pasa ktisis* occurs:

Mark 16: 15. 'Go ye into all the world, and preach the gospel to every creature' (*pase te ktisei*.)

Col. 1: 15. 'Who'—the 'dear Son' of 'the Father'—'is the image of the invisible God, the first born of every creature' (*pases ktiseos*). Ver. 23: 'If ye continue in the faith grounded and settled, and *be* not moved away from the hope of the gospel, which ye have heard; *and* which was preached to every creature' (*pase te ktisei*) 'which is under heaven.'

I Pet. 2: 13. 'Submit yourselves to every ordinance of man' (*pase anthropine ktisei*),—literally, to every human creature,'—'for the Lord's sake.'

In all these passages, *pasa ktisis* seems to be only applied to the human race, and therefore both *ktisis* and *pasa ktisis*, which plainly refer to the same thing, should be also so limited in Rom. 8: 20-22." *Genesis and Geology, by D. Crofton, B. A., and E. Hitchcock, D.D. L.L. D., p. 93-95. Whitby's comment upon Rom. 8: 20-23, refers it to the human race also.*

CHAPTER IX.

GEN. 1 : 24, 25, 26, 27, 28, 29, 30, 31.

"*And God said, Let the earth bring forth* (1) *the living creature after its kind, cattle and creeping thing, and beast of the earth after its kind; and it was so.*" "*And God made the beast,*" the wild animals, such as lions, tigers, bears, etc. ; especially all such as are carnivorous, "*of the earth after its kind.*" That is, God not alone created and contrived the different species of animals in all their variety of forms, instincts, and habits; but He also made them to produce each its own kind, and its own kind only, through all its successive generations. "*And the cattle after their*

•

----

1. "'Let the earth bring forth.' It is not to be supposed from this particular mode of expression that creative power was delegated to the *earth*, or that prolific virtue was imparted to the soil, to produce its own living tenants; for, in speaking of the actual execution of the work in the next verse, it is explicitly stated that it was God that created them, one and all. Omnipotence alone is adequate to produce living beings. *Spontaneous generation of life* is a thing unknown.—Every existing living organism has come from a parent, and every original parent came from the hand of God, for He alone can produce life."—*Dr. Morris, in The Terrible Catastrophe, or Biblical Deluge, etc., pp. 295, 296.*

kind," the various species of tame and domestic animals, such as sheep, oxen, horses, etc.,—all herbivor-
ous creatures. *"And everything that creepeth upon
the ground after its kind,"* such as serpents, frogs,
worms, etc. ; *"and God saw that it was good."*

"And God" after a solemn pause, having looked for
a model by which to frame man—this exquisite piece
of workmanship, and finding it in Himself, *said, Let us
(1) make man* (Heb. ADAM) *in our image, after our*

I. *"Let US make man;"* thus placing the origin of man outside the
chain of physical causation, and ascribing it to the immediate agency of
God. Besides, the creation here spoken of is the production of a *spiritual,*
not a material entity. God created man in *his own image.'* This creation
cannot be a formation out of a pre-existing matter, for no form of matter
can possibly bear any resemblance to God (Acts 17:29.) 'God is *spirit,'* and
man can be like God only in so far as he is endowed with a spiritual nature.
Spirit alone can bear the image of God. Whatever may be the teaching of
Genesis as to the origin of the human body, be it a formation,   *   *   *
there is no uncertainty in its language as to the origin of the human spirit.
It is an inbreathing from God. It proceeded directly from Him. By no
mere figure of speech, but by a Divine reality God is 'the Father of spirits,'
and man is the offspring and the image of God. This likeness of God lifts
man out of the sphere of mere nature—it sets him apart in the essential
characteristics and endowments of his being as *above* nature, and in some
sense *divine." Theistic Conception of the World, by Dr. Cocker, p.* 150.
    "That human souls are immortal, and that they do not perish with the
bodies, can be clearly and firmly established from the Holy Scriptures
alone. *Gerhard* produces the scriptural proof: 1. From the distinct assertion of our Savior, Matt. 10:28. 2. From the opposition of soul and body.
That in which soul and body are opposed to each other antithetically cannot in like manner be predicated of both. But immortality, soul and body
are opposed to each other in such a manner that mortality is affirmed of
the body, but denied concerning the soul. Therefore mortality cannot be
predicated of both in like manner, cf. Ecc. 12:7. 3. From the original creation of the soul. The souls of brutes were produced from the same material as their bodies, whence, when their bodies perish, the souls themselves likewise perish, Gen. 1:20. But into man he breathed a soul, Gen. 2:7,

likeness." (0) That is, let us make a being that will be free and self-conscious; that will resemble us intellectually and morally. (1) "*And let them have dominion over*" sublunary things, *the fish of the sea, and over the fowl of the air, and over the cattle, and over all the earth, and over every creeping thing that creepeth upon the earth.*" "*And God*" formed the body of

---

whence we thus infer: 'a soul whose origin is different from that of the souls of brutes does not have the same end with the souls of brutes.' But now the primeval origin of the human soul is different from that of the souls of brutes, because it was made not of an elementary material, as the souls of brutes, but divinely breathed into the body formed from the earth. Therefore, to the body there is ascribed *palsis* (the being moulded) from the dust of the earth, but to the soul the immediate *empneusis* (inspiration) of God. 4. From the name itself. * * The human soul is called spirit, Ecc. 3:21; Acts. 7:58; Hebr. 12:23. 5. From the continuation of life after man's death, Matt. 22:23; Mark 12:26; Luke 20:37; Hab. 1:12. 6. From the description of death, Gen. 25:8; 35:29; 49:33; Dan. 12:13; Acts. 26:18; Col. 1:12."— *Quenstedt, in The Terrible Catastrophe, pp. 332, 333.*

---

0. "Bei Mensch und Thier ist die Seele *Trager des Lebens*, daher als das Subject genannt, wo es Erhaltung, Rettung, Gefahrdung. Verlust, des Lebens gilt. * * * Die Seele vereinigt zunachst das ganze leiblich organisirte Leben in sich, und ist insofern, wie activ, so auch passiv, mit dem Leib und der sinnenwelt verbunden; wie das Leibesleben mit ihrem Daseyn steht oder fallt, so ist sie selbst wieder in ihrer Wirksamkeit und Zustandlichkeit abhangig vom Leiblichen. * * * In dieser Verwobenheit mit dem organischen Leben, auf welcher der ganze *sinnenwelt-liche Lebens*—Verkehr der Seele beruht, existirt und wirkt die Seele als *Odem* im Athmungsprocess (hebr. *Nacphaesch*, griech. *Psyche* lat. *Anima*); hierdurch ist eben das Thier und Menschenleben ein animalisches, athmendes, von dem blos vegetativen Stoffleben (der Pflanzen) unterschieden, und letzteres, das vegetative Leben, bei Mensch und Thier mit dem animalischen Leben zu Einem Organismus oder *Leibe* verknupft."

1. *Eph.* 4:24; *Col.* 3:10.

Adam out of the ground (1) and *"created"* the being of the creature life of *"man"* (HAADAM AYTH ELOHIM VAIYIBERAA) *"in his own image, in the image of God created"* (BARA) *"He him;"* to become His representative upon the earth.   For reasons stated in the following chapter, verse eighteen, *"male and female created He them;"* signifying at the same time that the race was to be constituted male and female. (2)   *"And God blessed them"*—gave them power to

---

"Die Menschenseele ist ursprunglich und wesentlich weder ein uberirdisches Geisteswesen, noch ein irdisches Sinnenwesen, sondern geschaffen durch das uberirdische Einwehen des goettlichen Lebensgeistes in den Koerperlichen Stoff, vereinigt sie in ihrer Odemsthatigkeit ein *Doppelleben, uberirdischgeistige Lebenskraft in sinnlicher Lebensform und Wirksamkeit.* (I. Mos. 2:7, vrgl. Pred. 12:7; 3:21; Jes. 57:16; Joh. 20:22; Hiob. 33:4.) Indem das Geistige bei ihr Durchaus verwebt ist in das Sinnenleben, unterscheidet sich der Mensch von dem Geistern; indem aber das Sinnliche wieder durchaus verwebt ist in hoeherer Geistigkeit, unterscheidet sich der Mensch von den Thieren, denen nur ein irdisches, leiblich belebtes Seelenwesen zukommt (I. Mos. 1:20, 24; vrgl. Pred. 3:21; Jer. 2:24.) Vermoege ihrer geis-

---

1.   "The preposition 'of' or 'out of,' is not authorized by the original. Dr. Whedon reads the whole passage as follows: 'And God developed' (VIA YITSER) 'the man—dust of the earth—and breathed into his nostrils the breath of lives, and the man became to a living person.' If the body of the second Adam, the Divine Man, was a birth (a miraculous birth), we do not see that anyone need be shocked at the suggestion that the body of the first Adam was also an extraordinary or supernatural birth."—*Dr. Cocker's Theistic Conception of the World, pp.* 165, 166.

2.   Just as God created the essence of the substances of the Universe at "The beginning," so to does He here create the essence or germs of mankind with the creation of the first man;—He "breathed into his nostrils the breath of *lives.*" "God created the whole human family in the loins of the first man—Adam; from whose substance Eve was made, **Gen.**

propagate and multiply upon the face of the earth.
"And" in virtue of this blessing *"God said unto them,
be fruitful, and multiply and replenish the earth,"* (1)
throughout all ages, *"and subdue it"* by cultivation,
exploration, and investigation, *"and have dominion*

---

tigen Lebens-Energie hat die Menschen-Seele *Natur und Kraft eines uber-
sinnlich lichten Selbst-Bewusstseyns und Erkennens* an sich, ist ein *goettlicher
Leucht-Odem* (Sprchw. 20:27; vrgl. Hiob. 32:8; 27:3, ff. I. Kor. 2:11; Luk. 11:35.)
Hierin liegt die Grundlage der moralisch intellectuellen Ausbildung des
Menschen und seiner Verklarung ins goettliche Leben, wenn die Seele
ihrem Lebensquell, dem Geiste Gottes, getreu bleibt und Lebenszufluss
daraus schoepft; eben so wird durch die Lichtnatur der menschlichen Seele
das ganze Sinnenleben des Menschen lichtartig (intelligent) bestimmt, und
der Leib erhalt seelischen Charakter (I. Kor. 15:44, 46, *soma phuchikon*
seelischer, Luther: naturlicher Leib.) Umgekehrt aber, wenn die Seele ihr
eigenthumliches Lebens-Element, die Gemeinschaft des goettlichen Geistes
verliert, und nur Lebenszufluss schoepft aus der sinnlichen Naturwelt;
erloescht auch ihre Lichtkraft im Sinnenwesen, die Seele selbst erhalt
einen sinnlichen, eiteln Charakter, und ihre uberirdisch geistige Lebens-
Energie erstirbt (Pred. 3:19-21; vrgl. 2 Petr. 2:12; Ps. 49:12 ff. Sprchw. 8:35, f.
Matt. 10:28.) Die *Geistigkeit* der Seele kann im Sinnlichen allmalig unter-
gehen, wie ihre Sinnlichkeit im Geistigen allmalig verklart aufgehen."—
Umriss der Biblischen Seelenlehre, von Dr. J. T. Beck, pp. 2, 3, 7, 8.

2:22, and in whom 'all have sinned,' Rom. 5:12; I. Cor. 15:22. This doctrine
is taught also by St. Paul, in his Epistle to the Hebrews, chapter seven:
verse ten; where Levi, the great grandson ot Abraham, is represented as
paying tithes to Melchisedec; while he, the remote descendant, to be born
two hundred and forty-six years later, was yet in the loins of Abraham."—
Evolution, as Taught in the Bible, etc., by Rev. G. C. H. Hasskarl, pp. 41, 42.
   "Eve was not co-ordinate with Adam, but represented in him   *   *
Eve was taken from Adam, but this was no new inbreathing from God.

---

   1. Jm 5 Kapitel, wo die Geschlechtstafel Adams verzeichnet ist, heisst
es im Anfang: 'Am Tage da Gott Menschen schuf, machte er sie in dem
Bilde Gottes. Man & Weib schuf er sie und segnete sie und nannte ihren
Namen Mensch, hebr. Adam, am Tage da sie geschaffen wurden.' Auch im
9 Kapitel, V. 6, wird noch einmal besonders hervorgehoben 'im Bilde Gottes

*over the fish of the sea, and over the fowl of the air,
and over every living thing that moveth upon the
earth."* (1) *"And God said, Behold, I have given
you every herb yielding seed, which is upon the face of
all the earth,"* that is, all the cereal plants, such as
wheat, corn, rye, etc., whose peculiar distinction and
characteristics are to produce seed; *"and every tree,
in the which is the fruit of a tree yielding seed; to you*

She was the emanation, so to speak, of the whole man—the effluence of his
body and soul, and the life of the whole race is that one united life. Eve is
called the *mother* of all living; but Adam is the *source* of all living, including Eve. There is then but *one human life in the world*—perpetuated and
extended through the generations—the emanation of the first life, that of
Adam."—*The Conservative Reformation and its Theology, etc., by Charles P.
Krauth, D. D., p. 381.*

"As Eve proceeded from out of Adam, so does the Church proceed from
out of the Second Adam (Gen. ii. 21-24), members of His body, being of His
flesh and of His bones (Eph. v. 30). Jesus Christ is called the Last Adam

hat er den Menschen gemacht.' Das also, worin alle Berichte uberein-
stimmen, ist die Gottes bildlichkeit, und zwar gab Gott ihm nicht bloss von
seinem Geist, es ist also nicht bloss von geistiger Ebenbildlichkeit die
Rede, sondern auch, wie der Wortlant zeigt, von physischer. Die Gottes
bildlichkeit bezeugt auch der Psalmist 8, 6: 'Du hast ihn ja nur wenig ger-
inger gemacht als Gott' und Jakobus 3, 9 nennt die Menschen 'nach dem
Bilde Gottes gemacht.'

"Nach diesen Berichten besteht nun der Mensch aus dem Erdenleib,
oder Fleisch und Gebein, dem von Gott eingehauchten Geist und der Seele.

---

1. Many of the species here created were afterwards preserved to the
world by the means of Noah's Ark alone. And that the animal species of
to-day have very materially diminished in size and form, from their prede-
cessors, need not surprise us, when we take into consideration the climatic
changes, that have wrought them;—the severity of the winter and the
excessive heat of the summer;—of which changes, the original creations
know nothing, for their climate was paradisiacal.—*The Author.*

it shall be for meat, (1) and to every beast of the earth, and to every fowl of the air, and to every thing that creepeth upon the earth, wherein there is life,"—that hath a living soul; "*I have given every green herb for meat; and it was so.*" That is, all grasses and succulent plants, whose nutritious qualities reside chiefly in the stems and foliage. "*And God saw every thing that He had made*" (AYTH KAL—all of the essence or

---

(I. Cor. xv. 45). Why is this name given to Him? As an afterthought, suggested by the First Adam? No. But *because the First Adam, in the very beginning, was instituted to be to the race natural what the Second Adam is to the race spiritual*, or the family of the redeemed; and, therefore, he is expressly called a figure or type of Him who was to come (Rom. v. 14)."—*Studies in the Creative Week, by George D. Boardman, D. D., pp.* 25, 26.

"If all the branches and twigs of the old trunk of humanity were germinally in Adam, the whole stock of the new manhood must be in Christ. He is the vine and we the branches. Each branch of the vine shall become

---

Aus dem oben angeführten Wortlaut I. Mos. 2, 7 folgt, dass der Mensch erst durch Gottesgeist-Verleihung ein Lebewesen, eine Seele wurde; die Seele hat also für sich erst Leben durch Geistes verleihung. Da aber auch den Tieren von der Schrift Seele, hebr. naphasch, zugeschrieben wird, so konnte man die seelische Gleich heit von Menschen und Tieren vermuten. Dies wurde ein Irrthum sein. Wie der Leib des Menschen durch einen besondern Schoepfungsakt Gottes gebildet ist, der des Tieres aber nich, so ist zwar die tierische Seele auch eine Erscheinung des schoepferischen Gottesgeistes, aber sie ist nicht wie die menschliche Seele der Erscheinung des dem Menschen unmittelbar durch Gott selbst eingehauchten Geistes. Dass

---

1. "In these words, God assigns, and points out to the newly-created man, the food suitable for him. It was plainly intended that he should subsist on vegetable food—herbs, grains, and fruits. These only were allowed to and used by man in his first estate. This abstinence from animal food is preserved in the traditions of all nations, as one of the characteristics of their golden age, or the age of innocence."—*Terrible Catastrophe,* p. 325.

substance created in "the beginning") "*and behold, it
was very good.*" "*And there was evening*"—the darkness which closed the fifth day, "*and there was morning*"—the light which introduced the next day, "*the
sixth day*". "*And the heavens and the earth were fin-
ished, and all the hosts of them.*"

"The first animals belong to the lower grades of the
aquatic fauna. As we ascend in the geological series, ver-
tebrate life has its commencement, beginning like the lower

a separate shoot, and itself a vine at the resurrection of the dead. But, before that event, each bud in the vine, in virtue of the fact that it is a bud,
must have an embodiment in the parent stock, a germinal body in the glorified
body of Christ."—*Gospel of the Resurrection. by Dr. J. M. Whiton, p. 266.
Quoted in "Evolution as Taught in the Bible," pp. 48, 49.*

aber der Geist nicht in der Seele aufgegangen, beweisen nicht wenige Stellen
der Schrift, z. B. Jes. 26, 9: 'Mit meiner Seele verlange ich nach dir bei
Nacht, ja mein Geist in meinem Innern such dich,' und der Psalmist bittet
51, 12: 'Und einen festen Geist erneuere in meinem Innern.' Der Apostel
schreibt 1. Thess. 5, 33: 'Und euer Geist ganz samt Seele und Leib musse
unstraflich behalten werden, etc.' Auch andere Stellen (1. Mos. 49:6; Ps.
7:6; 16:9; 30:13. Hebr. 4:12; Tit. 3:5.) beweisen ohne Frage die Selbststandig-
keit des Geistes und der Seele nebeneinander. Man wird demnach nicht
fehlgehen, wenn man die Seele als Tragerin und Vermittlerin des Lebens
ansicht, welches vom Geiste ausgeht; des halb sagt Tertullian: 'Die Seele
ist der Leib des Geistes, und das Fleisch ist der Leib der Seele.' Delitzsch
druckt dies so aus, dass er den Geist den Einhauch der Gottheit, die Seele
den Aushauch des Geistes nennt. Er sagt: 'Der Geist ist das Innere der

"Indem I. Mos. 2 das Seelenleben im Menschen aus Gott nicht durch
einen inneren Geistes process entsteht, sondern durch Leben anfachendes
Hauchen Gottes, durch einen freien, naturhaft heraustretenden Geistes
act: ist der menschliche Geist nicht als ein unmittelbarer Ausfluss aus dem
goettlichen Wesen dargestellt oder als ein Theil des goettlichen Seyns,
sondern als ein goettliches Werk (Sach. 12:1); anderer seits liegt im Hauchen ein aus dem inneren Wesen geschopfter Act, und so ist *der Menschen-
geist ein aus Gott frei herausgesetztes, einwesenhaft goettliches Princip in
geschoepflicher Existenz form;* daher kann gesagt werden Hi. 33:4: 'Geist

forms, in the waters, and represented at first only by the
fishes;   *   *   *   *   In like manner, the Scripture
record of creation, after stating the creation of lower forms,
goes on to specify the gigantic reptilian animals   *   *
termed *Tanimin*, and connects with them the birds, which,
with allied winged reptiles, were the contemporaries in
geological times.   (1)

"As we pass into the next creative æon, the Mammalia,
*   *   *   become dominant;   *   *   *   while
in the introduction of the beasts of the earth, or carnivorous mammalia, we have the inauguration of an era, the
later Tertiary, in which these assume the highest rank in

Seele und die Seele ist das Auszere des Geistes. Der Wesensbestand des
Menschen bestand also aus drei Konzentrischen Kreisen. Der innerste
war sein Geist, der innere seine Seele und der auszere sein Leib. Mit
seinem Geiste lebte und webte der Mensch in Gottes Liebe; der Leib stand
mittelst der Seele unter der Potenz dieses Liebeslichts und war von da aus
seiner Verklarung gewartig.' "—*Biblische Psychologie, Biologie und Pandaga-
gik, von Dr. Karl Fischer*, pp. 6, 7, 8.

Gottes hat mich gemacht, Odemswehen (Neschamah) des Machtigen belebt
mich.' Die Menschenseele entsteht nicht durch ein blos ausseres Befehls-
wort oder Machtwort aus dem Geist des allgemeinen Erdlebens (aus dem
goettlichen Naturgeist), wie die Thierseele (I. Mos. 1:20, 24, vrgl. 2), die, so
von unten stammend, nach unten wieder dahinfahrt, in das allgemeine
Naturleben wieder ubergeht Pred. 3:21 (daher keine individuelle Fortexis-
tenz); die Uranlage der *Menschenseele* wurzelt im Lebensgeist von obenher
(Pred. 12:7), in supranaturaler Lebenskraft vermœge des durch das goettliche Liebeswort von innen heraus vermittelten, goettlichen Geisteshauch
(I. Mos. 1:26; 2:7). *Es ist der goettlich-person hafte Geist, der Logos-Geist oder
der selbststandige, goettliche Vernunft-und Sprach-Geist, welcher in geschoepflicher Abbildlichkeit* (nicht in goettheitlicher Urbildlichkeit) *der menschli en*

---

1. "Das Koerperliche wird duch die Seele geistig individualisirt, wahrend
die ubrige Koerperwelt das Geistige nur im Ganzen als allgemeine Nutur-
kraft, nicht im Einzelnen als individuelle Lebens-Eigenschaft hat; eben so
wird das Geistige durch die Seele Koerperlich individualisirt, das heist,
leibhaft, wahrend es mit unbeselten Koerpern nich als seinen besondern

nature.   *   *   *   Lastly in this long procession,
Man appears, not the product of a separate day, but, in
accordance with the revelation of geology, at the close of
the same great period, in which the mammalia became dominant." (1)

"Not until we enter upon the Tertiary period do we find
flowers, amid which man might have profitably labored as
a dresser of gardens, a tiller of fields, or a keeper of flocks
and herds. Not, indeed, until late in this period is there
any appearance of several orders and families of plants
which are useful to man, and which contribute largely to

Seele immanent ist als selbststandiges Princip ihres Lebens (vgl. Joh. 1:4; 6:63;
20:22), daher der Mensch Sohn Gottes ist in real genetischen Sinn, in wesen-
hafter Gleichartigkeit (Luk. 3:38. Acts 17:28, f.). Aus dieser im goettlichen
Vernunft-und Sprach-Geist wurzelnden Uranlage eines selbstandigen
Geistes entsteht der menschlichen Seele zunachst ein Bewusstseyn von sich
als Selbst, *ein als Ich sich centralisirendes Selbst bewusstseyn,* wodurch sie
nach ihrem innerlichen Selbstseyn von allem ihr Zugehoerigen und sie
Umgebenden sich unterscheidet in Selbst beobachtung und Selbst erkennt-
niss," etc., etc.—*Umriss der Biblischen Seelenlehre, von Prof. Dr. J. T. Beck,*
pp. 10, 11.

Organen besonders verknupft ist, sondern nur sie als Theile Eines Ganzen
bewegt. Daher ist z. B. das Pflanzenleben theilbar, durch Trennung in
Ableger zu vermehren, wenn es nur mit der allgemeinen Naturkraft in
gesetz massiger Verbindung erhalten wird, weil die Pflanze als unbeseelt
Koerper und Lebensgeist nicht individuell in sich vereinigt; so bald sich
aber der Lebensgeist individuell dem Koerperlichen, und dieses sich
einverleibt, wie bei den Thieren, wird das Leben als Seelenleben bezeichnet,
(I. Mos. 1:30; Rev. 8:9), und seine Theilung fuhrt unvermeidlich theilweises
oder totales Absterben des Lebens mit sich."—*Biblische Seelenlehre, von*
Prof. Dr. J. T. Beck, p. 9.

---

1. *Dr. Dawson, in The Terrible Catastrophe or Biblical Deluge, etc.,* pp.
296-298.

his pleasure. Among these orders, we may mention that of the Rosaceæ, to which gardeners invariably look with unfailing interest. It includes the apple, the pear, the cherry, the plum, the peach, the apricot, the nectarine, the raspberry, the strawberry; nor ought we to omit reference to those delight-giving and useful flowers, roses and potentillas, the history of which commenced with that of man. It is no less remarkable that the true grasses, a still more important order, including the grain-giving plants, oats, barley, wheat and others which sustain at least two-thirds of the human species, and which also, in their humable varieties, form the staple food of the grazing animals, do not appear until close on the human period. There are other plants, also, which add to man's comfort or gratify his senses, which are not found in the fossil state—lavender, mint, thyme, hyssop, basil, rosemary, majoram. They have apparently been introduced to prepare for man their varied fragrance and virtues.

"There is distinct evidence of preparation for man in the distribution and adjustments of color, which alone must interest every student of the Bible and natural sciences. The very appearance of all things has been adapted to the human constitution."   (1)

"In whatever direction we survey the universe, we see that nothing is isolated, and no one thing exists without being adjusted to other things. All is in the most perfect harmony, and every thing perfectly answers the end for which

---

1. *Dr. Fraser, in Terrible Catastrophe, pp.* 325-327.

it was made. Creation is a book written by the finger of
God himself, and of which every page is filled to overflowing
with illustrations of His wisdom; it is a picture in which
His goodness is painted in colors of perfect truth; it is a
sculpturing in which His power is expressed in marvels of
form and harmony. Nothing that could be added, or that
could be withdrawn, would make creation more perfect
than this." (1)

Therefore well has America's greatest Geologist—Prof.
James D. Dana, said: "In this succession—from, first, the
lower animals, those that swarm in the waters, then creeping and flying species on the land; then beasts and cattle;
and lastly man;—we observe not merely an order of events,
like that deduced from science; there is a system in the arrangement, and a far-reaching prophecy, to which philosophy could not have attained, however instructed. The
record of the Bible is, therefore, profoundly philosophical in
the scheme of creation which it presents. It is both true
and Divine." And which closes with the remarkable an-
nouncement that God "blessed the seventh day, and hal-
lowed it; because in it He rested from all His work which
He had created and made." "Rested," how? "Rested,"
when? Did the planets cease to revolve and was the sun's
light extinguished? Did the earth again fall back into its
"waste and void" condition and was the darkness of the
"deep" to re-envelope it again? Were the fishes in the seas,
the flowers of field and meadow, the birds that fly in the
air, the beasts that roam over dale and hill and mountain

---

1. *Dr. Child, in the Terrible Cataastrophe, etc., pp.* 328-329.

together with man, the crown of creation,—created to breathe,—live and die,—all created for a moment, and then to perish and be no more? No! Never! *How* then did the living and ever active God rest? We reply, simply from the standpoint of the infant race. In fact, the whole account of creation is presented from the beginning to the end, as though man had been present, and had witnessed the various stages of the varied states of the development of the Universe and of the World. The early inhabitants, dwelling under and gazing at the stupendous greenhouse-roof which still canopied their earth, observed how that, because the rays of the sun could not penetrate the earth's surface, the clouds could not gather, the winds could not blow, a suspension must have taken place in the works of God. And it was because God ceased doing as he had heretofore,—seemingly caused a suspension in His works, that the infant race said, God "rested from all His work" in the Adamic age which prepared for the Noachian; in the Noachian which prepared for the Mosaic; in the Mosaic which prepared—indeed all of these together, for the Christian age; and the Christian for the most momentous and comprehensive of all the ages, the Resurrection Age.   (1)

TO THEO DOXA.

---

1. Unbelief, which is the wilful perversion of truths and facts, alone will gainsay the truths of the facts which are recorded in the foregoing account of creation as interpreted by the Scriptures.—*The Author.*

INDEX.

Abrahamic People, The page 5.

Adam, page 86; 88, Foot Note Also.

Animal Species of Noah's Ark, The page 90 Foot Note.

Archaean Age, The page 54.

Asah, page 17, Foot Note Also; 50; 75.

Astronomers, page 29; 38; 48.

Atheism, page 11 Foot Note.

Atmosphere, page 53, Foot Note Also.

Atom, page 15 Foot Note; 19 Foot Note; 21 Foot Note; 27.

Ayth, page 11; 18; 88.

Bara, page 11; 15; 16 Foot Note; 17, Foot Note Also; 18; 77; 82; 88.

Beast, page 85, ff.;

Behibaream, page 75.

Belief, page 7; 8; 21 Foot Note; 31.

Birds, page 77; 80, ff;

Bohu, page 30.

Book of God and Nature, The page 9; 77.

Carbon, page 47; 52 Foot Note; 53 Foot Note Also.

Change of Climate, The page 60; 65; 73.

Chaos, page 33, Foot Note Also.

Chemistry, page 13; 27, ff; 44 Foot Note.

Chemists, page 29.

Christian Age, The page 97.

Christian Fathers, The page 33 Foot Note.

Christian Religion, The page 39.

Chug, page 37, Foot Note Also.

Comets, page 47 Foot Note.

Continents, The page 63 Foot Note.

Cosmogony, The page 6, Foot Note Also.

Creation, The page 10, ff; 12 Foot Note; 15, ff; 17 Foot Note;
    18, Foot Note Also; 21; 33 Foot Note; 44; 46, ff; 78 Foot
    Note; 82; 85 Foot Note.

Darwinism, page 62 Foot Note; 80 Foot Note.

Dasha, page 59.

Day, Creative page 12 Foot Note; 42, Foot Note Also; 61; 73;
    75 ff.

Death, page 84 Foot Note.

Deluge, The page 31 Foot Note; 41, Foot Note Also.

Design, page 34; 67.

Doubt, page 7; 97.

Dry Land, The page 40; 49.

Earth, The page 11; 23; 25; 27; 32; 39, ff; 44; 47, ff; 51, ff;
    59, ff; Foot Note; 77, ff.

Elements, Creation Of The page 11; 18; 21; 25, ff; 28; 44, Foot
    Note Also; 45; 60 Foot Note.

Eminent Critics, page 17.

Errors, page 8,
Evolution, Theory Of page 20, ff; 78 Foot Note; 79 Foot Note.

Fatalism, page 12 Foot Note.
Firmament, The page 32, ff; 52, ff; 57; 83.
Fowl, page 77, ff; 90, ff.   .

Geologists, page 29; 48; 55 Foot Note.
Geschlechtstafel Adams, Die page 89 ff, Foot Note.
Glacial Age, The page 41 Foot Note.
God, page 11, ff; 16, ff; 21; 29; 31 Foot Note; 33 Foot Note;
     34; 44; 50, ff; 59, ff; 69, ff; 77, ff; 85, ff.
Goettlichen Seins, Willen, Wort, page 14, ff, Foot Note.
Gulf Streams, The page 41.
Granite, page 27; 53.
Grass, Herbs, etc., page 55; 59; 65.
Gravitation, The Law Of page 13; 14 Foot Note; 35 Foot
     Note; 70 Foot Note.

Haarets, page 11; 51,
Hashamajim, page 11; 51.
Heaven, page 11; 51; 59 Foot Note.
Human Soul, The page 86 Foot Note.

Jesus Christ, page 9, 31 Foot Note; 43 Foot Note; 46.

Language, page 5; 9; 14; 29; 32.
Law Of Circularity, The page 34 ff, Foot Note Also.
Laws and Forces of Nature, The page 14, ff; 16 Foot Note;
     21 Foot Note; 24; 34 ff, Foot Note; 44 Foot Note; 60 ff,
     Foot Note; 74 Foot Note.
Lauwrentian Period, page 54.

Liberty, Scientific, page 7; 21.

Life, page 34; 35 Foot Note; 38; 60 Foot Note; 62 ff, Foot Note; 72 Foot Note; 77, Foot Note Also; 79, Foot Note Also; 82.

Light, page 32; 42, Foot Note Also; 43 ff, Foot Note; 47; 51; 52 Foot Note; 57; 69, ff;

Light-Bearers, The page 69, ff; 72, ff; 74, ff.

Logic, page 9 Foot Note, 34, Foot Note Also.

Man, The Origin Of page 5; 9; 16; 17 Foot Note; 46; 86, Foot Note Also; 88, Foot Note Also.

Mammals, page 41, Foot Note Also. 93.

Materialism, page 12 Foot Note; 20 Foot Note.

Mathematical Relations, page 21 Foot Note; 26, ff.

Matter, page 13; 15; 16 Foot Note; 17 Foot Note; 19 Foot Note; 21, ff; 28; 32; 35 Foot Note; 39 Foot Note; 45 Foot Note; 52; 61 Foot Note; 66 Foot Note; 76 Foot Note.

Mearoth, page 69, Foot Note Also.

Measure, Numbers, etc., page 21 Foot Note.

Millenialism, page 38 Foot Note.

Mind, page 60.

Molecules, page 19, ff; 26.

Moon, page 32; 46.

Mountains, The Origin Of page 55 Foot Note; 56.

Nations, Genesis Of page 5.

Nebular Hypothesis, page 25; 51.

Nothing, From page 33, Foot Note Also.

Notes By The Author, page 6; 9; 12; 14; 19; 30; 31; 33; 34; 38; 41; 43; 44; 45; 52; 63; 76; 77; 80; 90; 97.

•

Oceans, The page 40; 59, ff.
Or, page 42, Foot Note Also.
Oxygen, page 53, Foot Note Also.

Pantheism, page 12 Foot Note.
Peat-Formation, page 48; 53.
Philosopher, page 5; 31.
Plants, The page 33; 38; 40; 47, Foot Note Also; 49.
Polytheism, page 11 Foot Note.
Principles, First page 10; 34 Foot Note.

Rakiya, page 50, Foot Note Also; 51 Foot Note.
Rathschlusse Gottes, page 15 ff, Foot Note.
Reason Of Man, The page 12 Foot Note; 31, Foot Note Also.
Record Of Genesis, page 10 Foot Note; 11; 77.
Reptiles, The page 83.
Resting of God, The page 96 ff.
Revelation, Its True Function page 10 Foot Note.
Ruach, page 30, Foot Note Also.

Schoepfung, Die page 13 ff, Foot Note; 87 ff, Foot Note.
Science, page 6; 7; 8; 10; 14; 19 Foot Note; 21; 70 Foot Note;
    74 Foot Note; 80 Foot Note.
Scriptures, The page 8, ff; 10; 15; 19; 32; 74.
Sea-Monsters, page 16; 77, ff; 80, ff.
Seas, page 40; 59 Foot Note Also; 77.
Seele, Die Menschliche page 87 ff, Foot Note; 92 ff, Foot
    Note.
Sin, Genesis Of, page 5.
Soil, The page 55, 65.
Solar Fire, The page 45, Foot Note Also; 46, ff.

Solids Of The Earth, page 25, ff.

Space. page 33; 45 Foot Note.

Spirit Of God, The page 11; 30, Foot Note Also; 43.

Sprechen Gottes, Das page 14 ff. Foot Note.

Stones Of Art. page 57 Foot Note.

Strata, page 37; 39, ff; 52, ff; 54, ff; 65, ff; 71, ff.

Substances, page 11; 13; 18; 25, ff; 37; 61 Foot Note.

Sun, The page 38 Foot Note; 45; 70 Foot Note.

Tertiary Period, page 94.

Theologian, page 5; 29.

Theories And Hypothesis, page 6.

Thohu, page 30; 51.

Thought, Liberty Of page 7.

Time, page 13; 19 Foot Note; 21 Foot Note; 33.

Truth-Defined, page 9; Its Relation To Thought 9 Foot Note.

Universe, The page 5; 9; 11; 13 ff; 21 Foot Note; 23; 29 ff; 35; 39 ff; 42; 44 ff; 70 Foot Note; 88 Foot Note.

Vav, page 31 Foot Note.

Vegetation, page 59 ff; 65 ff.

Vertebrates, page 81 Foot Note.

Volcanoes, page 56.

Weltall, Das page 13 ff, Foot Note.

Winds, The Trade page 41.

Word Of God, page 13; 18 Foot Note.

Writers, etc., page 5.

Yetser, page 17; 51.

Zones, page 41

EVOLUTION,

As Taught in The Bible.

ILLUSTRATED AND CORROBORATED BY

Spencer, Darwin, Huxley, Tyndall, Sayce, Muller, Virchow, Rousseau Agassiz, Herr, Dawson, Sweinfurth, Dana, Lyell, Peschel, Argyll, Miller, Brehm, Winchell, Baer, Humboldt, Wallace, Beale, Orton, Morse, Heckel, Mivart, Pfaff, Pasteur, Coleridge, Kant, Strauss, Janet, Reimensnyder, Morris, Campbell, Whitton, Quenstedt, Krauth, Marsh, Buckland, Œhler, Calorius, Boardman, Lewis, Drummond, Valentine, Thompson, Green, Hollazious, Keil, Shedd, Armstrong, Hickok, Delitzsch, Etc., Etc.

A PAMPHLET FOR THE TIMES,

BY

REV. G. C. H. HASSKARL, PH. D.,

Author of "The Word of God, Systematical and Daily,"
"The Terrible Catastrophe, or Biblical Deluge,"
"The Church's Triumph," etc.

PRICE, POSTAGE PAID, 25 CENTS.

WHAT IS SAID OF THE PAMPHLET:

I like the spirit of the work. . . It sustains the truth of the Bible.—PROF. JAMES D. DANA, LL. D., *Yale College, New Haven, Conn.*

The fundamental idea of the Pamphlet agrees with my own conviction.—PROF. DR. FRANZ DELITZSCH, *Leipzig University, Germany.*

The Pamphlet contains a large amount of valuable matter and useful references on the subject; besides a philosophical argument by the author, based on true principles of science, religion, and common sense.—PRINCIPAL SIR J. WM. DAWSON, C. M. G., LL. D., F. R. S., *President of the British Association.*

The author refutes—in a very courageous manner—not only all that which is implied in Darwinism; but, shows also how that it is contrary to Natural and Profane History.— PROF. DR. ED. KŒNIG, *Leipzig University, Germany.*

The arrangement of the Pamphlet is unique, the authorities quoted are the most eminent, and the logic and philosophy of the author's argument is irrefutable.   .   .
The Pamphlet stands alone in the field of literature.—REV. PROF. L. W. HART, A. M., D. D., *Brooklyn, N. Y.*

The Pamphlet commends itself very highly to every thinking mind.   .   .   Any person conscious of reason must enjoy the keen thrusts at the "philosophy of mud;" and every theist will catch inspiration from the emphasis given to the immanence of God in nature.   .   .   It is strong, very luminous and suggestive; revealing a tireless ardor in research and an enviable capacity for combining the fruits of investigation.—REV. NORMAN U. SKINNER, A. M., *of Union Theological Seminary, New York, N. Y.*

The Pamphlet is a very excellent production.   .   .
The author has thereby rendered a great service to the many clergymen who desire to stand aright on the many *isms* of the times, particularly the theory of evolution, which in our day has become the "pet" theory of so many. We most heartily recommend the Pamphlet to all who desire light upon this subject.—REV. F. P. BENDER, A. M., *Phila., Pa.*

The Pamphlet is a compend of scientific facts over against scientific assumptions.   The evolutionary origin of species is here crushed by an irrefutable array of authorities. It is such a *multum in parvo*, and in so cheap a form, that every defender of the Bible should have it.—REV. J. B. REIMENSNYDER, D. D., *New York City*.

The Pamphlet is written with much ability, illustrated by a familiar acquaintance with the literature of the theme. —B. K. PEIRCE, D. D., *in "Zion's Herald," Boston, Mass.*

The Pamphlet will be found a clearly put and quite useful defense of theistic evolution.—*The Moravian*.

There is only one kind of real evolution, and that we find revealed in Holy Scripture. True science can lead to no other result, as the author's skillful collocation of selections from writers of all shades of opinion strikingly illustrates.—PROF. CHAS. A. HAY, D. D., *Theological Seminary, Gettysburg*.

We not only admire the earnestness of the author with which he confronts the infidelity of natural philosophers; but also the decidedness with which he upholds the banner of Revealed Truth.—PROF. G. FRITSCHEL, D. D., *Mendota Theological Seminary, Ill.*

I am well versed on this subject; but yet consider this Pamphlet the ablest production. It is the most condensed and the most striking of all.—PROF. JOS. RECHTSTEINER, *Wagner College, Rochester, N. Y.*

A carefully prepared Pamphlet from a scholarly pen.— *Missionary Journal*.

The author has in a very ingenious way, and not unfair, ly, employed the concessions of the Evolutionists to show that species are fixed.   .   —*Herald and Presbyter-Cincinnati.*

It is a valuable work.   .   The testimonies are exceedingly forcible.   .   .   and must have taken the author years to accumulate.—*The National Baptist, Phila., Pa.*

The arrangement of materials and plan of treatment are very unique and interesting.   It will do good.—PRES. H. W.-MCNIGHT, D. D., *Pennsylvania College, Gettysburg, Pa.*

The impression which the Pamphlet makes is very favorable.—PROF. S. A. ORT, D. D., *Pres. of Wittenberg College and Seminary.*

It is of interest to read the views of a large and brilliant array of natural philosophers, who, without being second to any one in the knowledge of nature, distinctly pronounce against a theory, which by its charming plausibility abstracts the imagination, often interferes with sober judgment, and is calculated to antagonize the highest aspirations of the human mind.—PROF. W. J. MANN, D. D., *Philadelphia Seminary, Phila., Pa.*

This is really an interesting work, and will do good service.   .   .   It is on the right side, and brings the subject before the reader in a short space.—P. S. DAVIS, D. D., *in "The Messenger."*

Any person interested in the question, will admire the diligence of the author, and enjoy the freshness which he succeeds in maintaining throughout the whole discussion.—PROF. C. W. SCHAEFFER, D. D., LL. D., *in "The Foreign Missionary."*

The work is of great apologetical value.—PROF. J. D. SEVERINGHOUS, D. D., *Chicago Theological Seminary, Ill.*

I am profoundly pleased with the Pamphlet.—PROF. WM. J. SIMMONS, D. D., *Pres. of the Kentucky State University.*

The Pamphlet makes a very favorable impression.—PROF. M. LOY, D. D , *Columbus, Ohio.*

The Pamphlet is sensible, healthy and eloquent.—REV. T. B. ROTH, A. M., *Utica, N. Y.*

The citations are very incisive and interesting.—JOSEPH COOK, *Boston, Mass.*

The quotations are very much to the point, and are well grouped to strengthen the argument.—*The Workman, Pittsburg, Pa.*

Its abstracts from the authors named are to the point and all wisely used.—*Christian Standard, Cincinnati.*

In this interesting Pamphlet the author gives the Mosaic record of creation, and then cites the testimony of the most

eminent scientists and theologians of the world to confirm it. The Darwin theory of evolution is refuted by the highest scientific authorities. . . The subject is presented in a very compact and striking manner. , —
The Lutheran Observer.

The Pamphlet shows a wide range of reading on the part of the author. . . The Mosaic record that God made every plant and every animal to multiply or increase after its own kind *only* is shown to be in harmony with the universal experience and observation of mankind.—*Hartwick Seminary Monthly.* •

The Pamphlet . . illustrates and corroborates the plain sense of the Bible statement concerning Creation and the continual supply of life upon the earth. It is a little encyclopædia on the subject.—PROF. H. L. BAUGHER, D. D., *in "Augsburg Sunday-School Teacher."*

Send your order to the author, REV. G. C. H. HASS-KARL, or Lutheran Publication House, 42 North Ninth Street, Philadelphia, Pa.

THE TERRIBLE CATASTROPHE:

—OR,—

BIBLICAL DELUGE.

Illustrated and Corroborated by Mythology, Tradition and Geology, to which is Added a Brief Interpretation of the Creation, with Notes from Theologians, Philosophers and Scientists.

By Rev. G. C. H. Hasskarl, Ph. D.

Author of "The Word of God, Systematical and Daily."

12 Mo., Cloth pp. 384. Price, postage paid, $2.00.

The origin of the universe; the beginning of time and things; the creation of the angels and the origin of Satan, of heaven and earth; the beginning of the six days' creation; the origin of light before the sun; the definition of the word day, as used in the creative week; the appearing of dry land; the variety of trees, herbs and grasses that furnish and adorn the earth; the appointment of the two great lights; the existence of the moving creature that hath life; the making of beasts and animals; the creation of man in the Image and Likeness of God; the location and planting of the Garden of Eden; the primitive Ethiopia; the making of woman; the immortality of the soul, and how immortal; the question whether human souls are created daily, answered; the importance of the Tree of Life and the Tree of Knowledge of Good and Evil; the condition of man immediately after the creation; as well as *the preservation of one family, and the destruction of a sinful world;* the formation of the earth; the different strata; how, when and why the surface of the globe was changed; the varied fossils; when storms, volcanoes and earthquakes first made their appearance; the origin of rivers and mountains; how boulders were conveyed to distant places, and deserts originated; where animal and human remains are found, and where together; the caves in which domestic and war implements and graven pictures have been discovered; also, how Noah, his family, and all the animals were preserved; why the antedeluvians lived to an age that now seems incredible; and what the Myths and Traditions of all nations say concerning the Creation and the Deluge, are subjects of intense interest to all intelligent persons. In fact, these and a host of other questions, equally interesting and important, are answered in this volume.

The following are a few EXTRACTS from REVIEWS and LETTERS as to the character and merits of this work:

The matured opinions of the distinguished scholars are here presented in a form that is at once attractive and useful.—From PROF. C. W. SCHAEFFER, D. D., *Phila., Pa.*

The work has received very complimentary reviews from church papers, and is warmly commended by able scholars.—From *Indicator, of the Evang. Luth. Theological Seminary, Phila., Pa.*

The volume contains a great deal of important truth. . . The author is on the right side of the question.—From PROF. A. A. HODGE, D. D., LL. D., *Princeton, N. J.*

The author has certainly got together a strong body of arguments and authorities.—From *The Churchman, N. Y.*

The work is from an entirely new standpoint.—From *The Pastoral Visitor.*

The work is full of suggestive thought.—From PROF. M. VALENTINE, D. D., LL. D., *Gettysburg, Pa.*

The volume contains a vast amount of material new to many biblical students.—From *The Lutheran Observer.*

The author is an industrious reader, a thoughtful student, and a chaste and interesting writer, who has here collected from various sources many valuable facts.—From PROF. H. E. JACOBS, D. D., *in the Lutheran Review*.

— — —

There is a great mass of exceedingly interesting and curious material gathered together in this volume, which no one can read without profit.—From *The Workman, Pittsburg, Pa.*

— — —

The book is quite a store-house of illustrations and confirmations of Scripture statements drawn from all sources, heathen and Christian, ancient and modern, philosophical, scientific and religious. These illustrations and confirmations are so varied that some of them are quite plain to the most ordinary comprehension, whilst others will be appreciated by only the closely reasoning mind. The matter comprised in this book is calculated to dispel doubt, and to confirm simple faith. It is a valuable book for reference.— From H. L. BAUGHER, D. D., *Professor of the Greek Language and Literature in Pennsylvania College.*

— — —

The author gives to the Scriptural terms their most obvious meaning.—From *The Sunday-School World.*

— — —

The work has been prepared with painstaking care, and presents the results of an extended research in a clear and instructive way. It shows how fully science has confirmed the Bible, and will help to dispel doubts, and fortify believers against the objections of cavilers.—From PROF. W. H. MC-NIGHT, D. D., *President of Pennsylvania College, Gettysburg, Pa.*

The author has grappled with his subject with giant strength.—From *The Lutheran Evangelist, Springfield, O.*

An appalling list of authorities has been consulted.—From PROF. E. J. WOLF, D. D.

Whatever may in any wise be brought in connection with the subjects, or imagined to have such connection, is here discussed.—*The Lutheran.*

We are astonished at the amount of information the author has brought together on this all important subject.—From PROF. A. SPAETH, D. D.. *Philadelphia Seminary.*

The Terrible Catastrophe is a work of great value, and one that will commend itself to ministers, teachers, and the educated generally.—From PROF. H. H. BROWNMILLER.

The work is a valuable contribution to literature.—From PROF. THOS. G. GENTRY, M. A., *Phila., Pa.*

Mr. H. has certainly brought a good deal of earnest study to bear on his book. To explain it satisfactorily, and to gather this evidence from mythology, tradition and geology, and place in it clear strength before the modern reader, has been the object of the book produced.—From *The Times, Philadelphia, Pa.*

The impression which Rev. Mr. H.'s work on *The Ter-rible Catastrophe* makes is, that whenever it may be thought that either science or the Bible may be mistaken, the reader may rest assured that the mistake will be found on the part of science. His work is new, original, scientific and Scriptural; and an invaluable treasury in every library.—From *The Middletown Press.*

This volume (*The Terrible Catastrophe*) deserves to be in every family, school and seminary library. We know of no work in any language, in all the bounds of sacred and secular literature, which is calculated to exert a more wholesome and beneficial influence on young and old than this work.—From *Harrisburg Telegraph.*

Send your order to the author, REV. G. C. H. HASS-KARL, or Lutheran Publication House, 42 North Ninth Street, Philadelphia, Pa.

THE CHURCH'S TRIUMPH

—IN THE—

FORMATION AND ADOPTION

—OF THE—

AUGSBURG CONFESSION,

TOGETHER WITH NOTES FROM

The Most Eminent Authorities:

—AND A—

Complete Analysis of the Confession By

REV. G. C. H. HASSKARL. PH. D.

*Author of "The Word of God, Systematical and Daily," "The Terrible Catas-
trophe, or Biblical Deluge," "Evolution as Taught in the Bible," etc.*

Price, 25 Cents.

· WHAT IS SAID OF THE PAMPHLET:

The History of the Confesssion is excellent.—PROF. S. A.
ORT, D. D.

The Pamphlet is an able and excellent work.—REV. H.
C. HOLLOWAY, D. D.

The Pamphlet is deserving of wide circulation.—REV.
PROF. J. RECHTSTEINER.

The Pamphlet is deserving of many thoughtful readers.
—Prof. W. J. Mann, D. D., LL. D.

The Pamphlet is well adapted for general circulation among the people.—*The Lutheran Observer.*

We welcome the Pamphlet with joy. The analysis is excellent.—Prof. M. Guenther, St. Louis, Mo.

The Pamphlet is highly appreciated by the Professors and Students of our Seminary.—Prof. Chas. A. Hay, D. D.

The History of the Confession is accurate, and the analysis of the articles is simple.—Prof. F. Lutz, *in Kirchenblatt, Iowa.*

The Pamphlet contains valuable extracts in foot notes from eminent authors.—Prof. M. Loy, D. D., *in Lutheran Standard.*

The Pamphlet is interesting and instructive, indicating careful research, sound judgment and a fervent spirit.—Prof. C. W. Schaeffer, D. D., LL. D.

Many a pastor will, in spirit, gratefully clasp hands with the author for the most excellent analysis;—for enabling him to grasp firmly the doctrinal contents of each article.—Prof. S. Fritschel, D. D.

The introduction is so good, and the analysis so simple, that we are well persuaded that this treatise merits and we hope it may receive wide circulation.—B. M. Schmucker, D. D., *in The Lutheran.*

"The Pamphlet will prove very convenient and useful to those who are anxious to have in a concise form an outline of the history and the contents of our precious Augustana."—Prof. A. Speath, D. D.

I heartily recommend the Pamphlet to every Lutheran family in the land. There is nothing like it in the English language. . . I hope that edition will follow edition in quick succession.—Rev. A. C. Wedekind, D. D.

The Analysis ought to be very serviceable not only to English but also to German readers, for the clear comprehension of the confessional and doctrinal kernel; for, the more exact and sharp conception of its contents is essentially facilitated.—Prof. G. Fritschel, D. D., *in Kirchliche Zeitschrift.*

It was with great pleasure and interest that we have read this Pamphlet. . . It certainly required careful reading and systematic study on the part of the author to be able to present and treat the subject with such skill. . . We hope that it may soon be found in every Lutheran family.—*Indicator of the Philadelphia Theological Seminary.*

The Pamphlet is interesting and accurate. . . It is well calculated to accomplish the end at which the author aimed in its preparation, viz: "to set forth more

prominently and clearly the doctrines that have always inspired the life of the Christian Church; and to awaken a new
interest in the priceless treasures that are the heritage of the
Lutheran Church."—*The Workman.*

The analysis of the Augsburg Confession, is in my mind,
the most complete compendium of the text of that illustrious
Confession that I have ever seen.   I have read it over several
times with interest and great satisfaction.   .   .   The
Pamphlet contains an array of authorities and a range of
investigation that impress me with the patient and diligent
research which the author had to undergo to bring forth
such a valuable production.—Rev. A. W. Lilly, D. D.

Send your order to the author, Rev. G. C. H. Hasskarl, or Lutheran Publication House, No. 42 North Ninth
Street, Philadelphia, Pa.

The Sanctuary,

ITS ORIGIN, DESIGN AND IMPORTANCE:

—OR—

Reasons Why Sanctuaries are Necessary, the Style of Architecture which the Lutheran Church Should Observe, and the Territory wherein Lutheranism should Expand to its Grandest Future.

BY REV. G. C. H. HASSKARL, PH. D.,

Author of "The Terrible Catastrophe or Biblical Deluge," etc.; "Evolution, as Taught in The Bible;" "The Church's Triumph," etc.

——PRICE, POSTAGE PAID, 15 CENTS.——

WHAT IS SAID OF THE ADDRESS:

The Address is published by request of Synod—which pronounces it an "able and exhaustive Address on Church Extension," and this judgment the author well sustains.— *The Lutheran Observer*.

———

The Address is excellent. It couldn't be better. It is not only well wrought out, but very suggestive.—REV. H. H. WEBER, *General Secretary of the Board of Church Extension of the General Synod of the Evang. Luth. Church.*

The Address is excellent, full of useful instruction concerning the uses and adaptations of houses of worship, etc. The pains-taking author has done himself credit, as he always does in his researches and literary productions.—REV. M. SHEELEIGH, D. D., *in the Lutheran Sunday-School Herald.*

———

I have read the Address with much pleasure and profit. It is an earnest and stirring plea in the interest of Church Extension, and its reading ought to effect a deeper interest in the work of Home Missions. You have put the Church under many obligations for the faithful presentation of this subject.—REV. D. M. KEMERER, *President of Home Missions in the Pittsburg Synod.*

———

In this timely Address the author stirs his hearers to a realization of the necessity of erecting church buildings for the purpose of worship. He adduces arguments from history, from God's command, from actual results, from incidental results, in support of his position, etc.—*The Lutheran.*

———

I read the truths, so well and truthfully presented, with much interest; and hope they may work, with the divine blessing, for the end had in view; the extension of the Great Redeemer's Kingdom.—REV. PROF. F. A. MUHLENBERG, D. D., LL. D., *President of the Board of Home Missions of the Ministerium of Pennsylvania.*

———

The Address will convince the most skeptical that it is not sufficient to worship God amid the trees of the forest and beneath the blue dome of the world's cathedral, but that the Holy Scriptures intimate, both by the most ancient practice of the Jews and by the direct command of God, that becoming sanctuaries should be erected, wherein God may be publicly and appropriately worshipped.—*Indicator of The Theological Seminary of Mt. Airy, Philadelphia, Pa.*

———

Your sermon is well conceived and well executed. It is logical in its arrangement; and its arguments, whether historical, or mandatory, or practical are clear and to the point. I like your idea about Gothic style, as being eminently suitable to our own worship.—REV. PROF. C. W. SCHAEFFER, D. D., LL. D.

———

I need not say, that the missionary spirit, from which your address emanates, meets with my hearty approval.— REV. PROF. W. J. MANN, D. D., LL. D.

———

Your Address bears reading, once and again; it gains thereby.—REV. PROF. L. W. HART, *Brooklyn, N. Y.*

———

Send your order to either the author, REV. G. C. H. HASSKARL, or Lutheran Publication House. 42 North Ninth Street, Philadelphia. Pa. *Veil.*